Invisible Girls

THE TRUTH ABOUT SEXUAL ABUSE

DR. PATTI FEUEREISEN *with Caroline Pincus*

Seal Press

Invisible Girls THE TRUTH ABOUT SEXUAL ABUSE

Published by
Seal Press
An Imprint of Avalon Publishing Group, Incorporated
1400 65th Street, Suite 250
Emeryville, CA 94608

AVALON
publishing group incorporated

In order to protect the privacy and honor the confidentiality of Dr. Feuereisen's clients, all names used in this book have been changed, as have identifying details (school names, ethnicities, numbers of siblings, geographical locations, etc.). While the girls' prose was occasionally edited for grammar and flow, their stories are all true.

Library of Congress Cataloging-in-Publication Data

Feuereisen, Patti.

Invisible girls : the truth about sexual abuse / Patti Feuereisen ; with Caroline Pincus.

p. cm.

ISBN-10: 1-58005-135-9

ISBN-13: 978-1-58005-135-4

1. Sexual abuse victims—United States. 2. Teenage girls—Abuse of—United States. 3. Sexual abuse victims—Rehabilitation—United States. I. Pincus, Caroline. II. Title.

HV6592.F48 2005   362.76'082—dc22   2004030252

9 8 7 6 5 4 3

Cover design by Gia Giasullo, studio eg
Interior design by Domini Dragoone
Printed in the United States of America by Malloy
Distributed by Publishers Group West

To my daughter, Aviva,

and to Caroline's daughter, Ruby,

and to *all* daughters everywhere.

Acknowledgments

Of course, the first people to thank are my beautiful clients, the hundreds of young women whom I have been blessed to work with through the years. And all the young women I have met at my workshops. Their courage and brilliance are effervescent and inspiring.

Then I need to thank Caroline Pincus. She is the extraordinary midwife of this book, and my new dear friend. She brought my words to life. I thank her family, Esther and Ruby, for their support of giving up precious time with Caroline! I thank my agent, Loretta Barrett, for her unwavering support and faith, and for bringing me Caroline. Also thanks to Gabe and Rick at Barrett Books. I thank my circle of women friends for their deep friendship and for always being there: Candy Talbert, Connie Grappo, Jane Dorlester, Mary Walker, Mary Krauss, Robin Kahn, Liz Hoffman, Pam Wheaton, Tracy Gilman, Elizabeth Haase, and my newest friend Toni Iacolucci. A special thanks to Serena Schrier, who was there from the beginning and massaged me through the process.

Thanks to Lyn Mikel Brown for her openness and early read and great collegial networking. Also thanks to Kay Jackson for her early read and steady support. Thanks to Joan Bossert at Oxford Press for her deep belief in this project. A special thanks to all the women at Seal Press who supported this project with understanding and excitement: Ingrid Emerick for initial editorial support, Krista Rafanello for fabulous encouragement and public relations work, Krista Lyons-Gould for extraordinary sensitivity and understanding, Jane Musser for her patience and perseverance on the cover design, Denise Silva for helping form the Resource Center section, and last, Avalon's President, Susan Reich, for her immediate positive response and belief in the project. I thank all the wonderful students and staff at Edward R. Murrow High School for their participation in this project. A special acknowledgment to Mr. Kingston, Ms. Wachtel, Mr. D., Mr. Abdul-Wali, and Ms. Pindar for being so open to the thoughts and feelings of teenagers and sexual abuse.

I thank my daughter Aviva for being such an amazing daughter and adolescent girl extraordinaire. She is a constant source of love and pride. Last, I thank my anchor, my husband Mark, for his love, devotion, and support, and for being the best man I know.

. . . and from Caroline . . .

Collaboration, at its very best, enriches not only the final product but all the people involved in getting it there. That has certainly been true for me in the writing of *Invisible Girls*. I am deeply grateful to Patti Feuereisen for nudging me to step into the shoes of cowriter (although I have been editing books for over twenty years, this is my first true cowriting venture) and to our agent, Loretta Barrett, for introducing us in the first place. From the moment Loretta showed me an early draft proposal for this book, I knew that I wanted to work with Patti. She is an extraordinary and courageous woman, and I am honored to have had a part in bringing this important book to life.

I am also grateful to the wonderful women at Seal Press for their commitment to books that the "big boy" publishers are afraid to touch—books that offer girls and women genuine support for taking their power.

I thank Patti's family for sharing her with me these past few years and for bringing their own formidable creative juices to the project. And finally, I thank my daughter Ruby for being deliciously five and my wife, Esther, whose love for and belief in me is something of a miracle.

Welcoming Pandora

My Take on the Ancient Greek Myth

According to Greek myth, Pandora was the first woman, like Eve of Hebrew mythology. She is said to have received many, many gifts from the gods—hence her name, Pandora, which means "all gifted" or "all gifts." Aphrodite gave her beauty; Apollo gave her musical talent and a gift for healing; Hermes gave her a box and told her not to open it. Then he gave her curiosity!

Here she was, holding this beautiful box that she had been ordered not to open. A smart and energetic woman, in defiance of the patriarchy, she opened the box. Out spilled all the great misfortunes of the world, including the pain of all the girls and women who had ever been sexually abused.

Others might have feared letting such troubles out of the box, but Pandora knew that when you keep a box closed, you also close off hope. She knew that hope lies in opening the box, in revealing the truth, in releasing the trauma. She was not afraid. She knew that girls are healed every time women's sexual trauma is let out of its box and released into the world.

I invite all of you to join me in opening Pandora's box.

Table of Contents

PART FOUR
THE ROAD BACK

Welcome

Thank you for picking up this book. One out of four young women in the United States will be abused by the time she is sixteen. This book is for all of you. Please know that whoever you are, you are not alone!

If you are a survivor, I want to offer you a special welcome. Whether you are already hard at work healing from the trauma of abuse or are just admitting for the first time—perhaps even to yourself—that you were abused, I hope you will find this book to be an important step in your healing process.

This book is filled with survivors' stories, and they may trigger some intense feelings and painful memories for you. Please feel free to skip around and take the book in the doses you can handle. You might want to keep a journal to record your thoughts, feelings, and memories. If you're not currently in counseling, we hope you will find someone you can trust with whom to share the feelings that come up for you as you read.

If you don't have someone you can talk with, or cannot find immediate support, or aren't ready to talk openly with someone in your own community, please know that you can always call the national hotline for rape and incest survivors (RAINN) at (800) 656-HOPE (800-656-4673), or you can write to me personally at our website, www.girlthrive.com, which I set up as a companion to this book.

Invisible Girls also opens up sexual abuse to the community and to the culture at large. It offers a porthole into the worlds of teenage girls and young women who are abuse survivors. You have never heard the voices of young survivors in quite this way before. To clinicians and medical professionals; parents; high school and university guidance departments; students of psychology; personnel at rape crisis centers and at adolescent and

ric units; high school and college psychology classes;
s and relatives of abusers: *Invisible Girls* will lead you to
to a deeper understanding of sexual abuse and help you to
culture of shame and secrecy that surrounds abuse.

twenty years of working with sexual-abuse survivors, I have
ped being amazed by the ingenuity and brilliance of girls, by their
to thrive even through horrible experiences. I learn so much from
. I learn how they have coped, how they've found comfort in the
ld, how they've moved on in their lives and found good, healthy love.
these girls are my teachers, and now some of them have come forward to
share their journeys with you.

The stories, quotes, questions, and poetry included in this book were
contributed by some of the hundreds of girls I have worked with over the
years. These are girls I know personally, and I want you to know them, too,
and to grow and learn from their strength and their experiences. They are
all grateful for the opportunity to reach out to you. In order to ensure
their privacy and safety, however, I asked them to choose pseudonyms.
With perfect synchronicity, some girls asked if they could be called by
gem names, others flowers, and I realized how perfect that was—that they
would be seen in all their brilliance and beauty and radiance: Zinnia, Lily,
Coral, Garnet, Topaz, Sage, Ivy, Amber, Jasmine, Iris, Dahlia, Pearl.

In my eyes, every one of these girls—and every other sexually abused
girl who finds her voice, finds someone to whom she can tell her story—is
a heroine. Whether or not you are a survivor, we invite you to join these extraordinary girls in their movement to end the silence, to release the
shame and guilt and fear, and to begin the healing of the collective spirit
of girls everywhere.

Introduction

"When I was twelve years old, my father explained that I was a
beautiful young girl, and that he had to have me because he was
a hungry man. He said that one could not put a plate of
spaghetti in front of a hungry man and expect him not to eat it."

—A TWENTY-TWO-YEAR-OLD INCEST SURVIVOR

The girls you are about to meet are not the girls we typically think of
when we hear the words "sexual abuse." Like you, they are normal girls—
highly functioning and high-achieving—girls on the soccer team, the debate team; girls at top prep and public high schools; girls destined for top
colleges, as well as young women already in college and those starting careers.
They come from upper-, middle-, and working-class backgrounds. They are
of European American, Asian American, Latin American, and African
American descent. They are Jewish, Buddhist, and Christian. Girls you'd
"never think" had been, or were being, abused. I call them invisible girls
because they defy our stereotypes. And the fact is, no one can tell from
the outside whether or not you have experienced sexual abuse.

Throughout this book, you will hear directly from girls who have endured sexual abuse. They will tell their stories of incest, date rape, acquaintance rape, and mentor abuse. All too often, as you'll see, they wonder
"Why me?" or "Why didn't I stop him?" Even today, there is still so much
cultural denial, so much personal guilt and shame surrounding the subject
of abuse, that girls often feel it is their fault.

"When you live in the same house with a predator, your sixth

sense is alive and kicking at all times. You know he is going to do something that night, even before he considers what is at stake. The fight is only on the surface, a delicate exchange of looks, of using the other bodies around to try and plan your escape. It's futile and you know it. In the Disney story, Bambi had a chance, the chance of running as fast as he could in the open field. That doesn't mean he will make it, but he can run. I didn't know I could, because no one had shown me how to. It would take me a while to learn—after all the harm was done."

—A TWENTY-TWO-YEAR-OLD INCEST SURVIVOR

Boys Will Be Boys

Why didn't you stop him? This is a question that survivors of sexual abuse ask themselves all the time. But there are very good reasons why you didn't stop him. You didn't stop him because you lived under "his" roof; because you depended on him financially; because your abuser wove a web of fear and entrapment around you; because you were confused; because you were young and didn't have good options or a strong support system in place. This book will help you work through these feelings of entrapment and fear to see that sexual abuse is never your fault, and that you did nothing to cause your own abuse.

Why didn't you stop him? You didn't stop him because we live in a culture where "boys will be boys"—a culture that, through its fairy tales, movies, and advertising persistently pushes the sexist belief that young girls are ready for sex when their bodies first develop; a culture that insinuates that these girls "really want" the older men who abuse them; a culture that still questions the victim's role in the crime, whether it be a young girl raped by her uncle ("Was she being flirtatious?"), or a guy who rapes his date ("Was she leading him on? What was she wearing?"). We live in a culture in which a male-dominated government decides the laws about rape and incest, pornography, child and spousal abuse, and abortion—laws that directly impact women's health and happiness. Simply put, we live in a culture that does not honor women and children; where sexuality, especially

4

female sexuality, is a commodity, something that is used to sell products or satisfy male desires; where women, and especially women of color, are depicted on music videos as little more than prostitutes. In this culture, men still sexually abuse girls at staggering rates.

The Historical Cover-up

The shameful fact is, forced sexual contact without consent—from inappropriate touching to sodomy to rape—has been with us throughout history and wasn't even widely acknowledged as a crime in the United States until women in the 1970s began to speak out. As far back as the late nineteenth century, the father of modern psychiatry, Sigmund Freud, made efforts to publicize the trauma of incest. He had become increasingly disturbed as patient after patient—affluent women from conventional families—described sexual abuse at the hands of their fathers, uncles, family friends, or male relatives. At first he took these women at their word and rushed to present his startling findings to his colleagues (some of whom, it is now known, were molesting their own patients and nieces). He was roundly ridiculed and harshly rebuked in the professional community. In order to redeem himself, he "rethought" the whole issue and decided that these women had only fantasized about the abuse—that their accounts were nothing more than an elaborate wish to be forcibly taken by their fathers, uncles, even their therapists! This is what has come to be known as Freud's "seduction theory," and it set a precedent for disbelieving victims of sexual abuse for the next hundred years.

The Feminist Uncovering

Yet in the 1970s, women started speaking out about their incest and abuse experiences, and feminist clinicians followed. Freud's theories were challenged and criticized within the medical field. And with the work of pioneering scholars like Judith Lewis Herman and Diana Russell, as well as the publication of Sandra Butler's *Conspiracy of Silence* and Louise Armstrong's personal memoir of incest, *Kiss Daddy Goodnight,* the silence and disbelief around incest and abuse slowly broke open. But it wasn't until the publication of Ellen Bass and Laura Davis's *The Courage to Heal* in 1988 that the issue really took the spotlight. In this book, dozens of women spoke about the ongoing trauma of the sexual abuse they had experienced as children. The book gave women permission to believe in themselves in a most profound way.

But, invaluable as all these books are, all of them told the story of abuse from an adult's perspective.

In the 1990s, adolescent girls and young women started writing their own books. They wrote about love, life, family, sex, drugs, depression, and eating disorders. Sara Shandler's *Ophelia Speaks* is the best-known example. Then girls who had been sexually abused started publishing zines and writing songs about it. Now in our book, you will hear not only their stories of sexual abuse, but also of their healing, in their own words.

The fact is that girls and young women are brilliant and resilient and can heal from sexual abuse. When survivors are given the opportunity to talk about their abuse in a safe environment, to let go of confusing feelings of shame and guilt and self-blame, they have every chance of healing and of realizing wonderful, satisfying lives and relationships as adults.

Talk about it now. If you hold your abuse inside you into your twenties, thirties, forties, and beyond, it can deprive you of healthy, loving relationships and self-esteem, because you never get the chance to process the shame and the secret. As survivors discover time and again, not telling can mean living in a perpetual state of fear and mistrust and an inability to have trusting sexual relationships. Not talking about it can mean not feeling safe in the world. And keeping it secret can prevent you from embracing the love and joy that are your birthright.

Don't Wait to Tell...

Liz, a thirty-four-year-old incest survivor, left home at nineteen, marrying the first man who asked her to. That marriage lasted about fifteen years, until he beat her so badly she was hospitalized. During the hospitalization, Liz began having vivid flashbacks of her early childhood sexual abuse and was eventually referred to me. It took her several months to reveal to me that she was a survivor of sexual abuse. She had never told anyone.

Another client, Shari, a thirty-year-old social worker who had survived incest throughout her adolescence, had held her secret tightly, too, and she was on her second divorce from an abusive man when she attempted suicide.

Marilyn was referred to me after a hospitalization for clinical depression. She was an attorney. She'd been having nightmares since her stepfather raped her at fourteen. She finally had a breakdown at age forty-three.

Suzanne, fifty-two and a high school teacher, was also an incest survivor. She came to see me in the middle of her divorce because her fifteen-year-old daughter was being molested by her husband.

Joanna, a thirty-six-year-old artist, couldn't sleep because of recurring nightmares. She had survived a rape during her freshman year in college and had never told anyone.

I've treated women who've suffered through years of migraine headaches, nausea, memory lapses, failed relationships, thoughts of suicide, drug and/or alcohol abuse—all problems stemming from a history of sexual trauma. Through friendships, college, jobs, and relationships, these women kept their secrets tucked away in a safe place and tried to forget about them. But as they eventually discovered, forgetting doesn't work.

Working with women in their thirties, forties, fifties, and sixties convinced me that I had to do whatever I could to help young survivors heal from their abuse so they wouldn't have to endure years of torment.

As younger clients started to come in to my practice and talk about their abuse, there was a different quality to their disclosure. There was always hope underneath their pain; their abuse had not had enough years to dig itself into their souls. So in 1993, when a few of my teenage clients told me they wanted to start a survivors' group, I jumped at the chance. I organized a group that met in my office, and to reach out to an even larger community, of girls, I began running pro bono workshops about sexual abuse at one of the top high schools in New York City. The girls put up posters for the group in the bathrooms, and soon I had a vibrant group of girls in a racially, socially, and ethnically diverse high school of three-thousand-plus students.

One of my most effective techniques for helping girls in these groups to open up is to have them write out their questions and experiences anonymously on index cards and then read each other's cards aloud. The experience is never short of phenomenal. Hearing other girls' questions and comments unlocks the floodgates of long-held secrets:

"I survived rape last year, but I've never told."

"My cousin molested me when I was six. I never told."

"How can I protect my little sister? I think my father is messing with her the way he did with me."

"My boyfriend forced me to have sex; I said no. Was I raped?"

"My parents are divorced now, but my father abused me. I never told my mom or anyone."

"I am having nightmares about when my cousin molested me. I never told anyone. I am afraid of what will happen."

As one girl told another, and then another, a kind of underground network of girls from other area high schools and colleges brought more and more girls to my workshops, support groups, and counseling sessions. Pretty soon I was seeing hundreds of survivors. The more they talked, the stronger and more confident they became.

And what I witnessed over and over again was that as these girls found a safe place to talk, they began to speak of their experiences, and as they spoke of their experiences, they began to heal. One young woman said, "I sealed myself off. I figured if everything looked okay from the outside, maybe the inside would eventually change, but it never did until I admitted what had happened to me and stopped hiding." Another said, "I used to tell myself it never really happened, but when I started talking and I faced it, it became smaller and smaller, and so did my father." And another: "When I began to tell, it was like I had jumped off a freight train and had finally reached my destination."

In situation after situation, what I witnessed convinced me that it is far easier to come to terms with sexual trauma during adolescence and early adulthood than later on in life. It makes sense. We are at our most resilient during these times; we're still growing and changing. If you can talk about trauma while you're still young, still figuring out who you are, it simply can't plant its roots as deep. You see, it's the secrets that really do us the most harm. In all these girls, I felt an urgency to get better and a resilience that simply was not present in the older women who had let their abuse eat away at them for ten, twenty, thirty years.

The Birth of Our Book

Invisible Girls was conceived from this urgency. My experiences with these girls made me realize that the sooner these young woman acknowledged the abuse and let go of their closely held secrets, the sooner, and more completely, they would heal. It was the girls I worked with who urged me to publish their stories and experiences. They wanted to reach out and create a great circle of girls and young women speaking out, supporting each other, healing.

According to the U.S. Department of Justice's Bureau of Justice Statistics for 1997, 44 percent of rape victims are under the age of eighteen, and young women aged sixteen to twenty-four are the most vulnerable to sexual violations by intimate partners. In spite of a persistent underreporting of incest and other sex crimes, the statistics for sexual abuse of adolescent girls and young women are simply staggering. Girls who have been through the experience deserve to be heard and to hear from one another. I wrote this book to give voice to the voiceless.

I also wrote it to help girls and young women who have not been abused become aware of the realities of sexual abuse, to become smarter and safer as they come into their sexuality, and stronger and more resilient in the face of a culture that still defines girls and women by how well we satisfy the needs of men.

The wonderful girls and young women who speak in this book share their experiences of ongoing sexual abuse within their families, as well as of one-time abuse by an uncle or cousin or family "friend." You will learn about acquaintance rape, date rape, and stranger rape, and the specific emotions and issues that tend to arise from each situation. For example, in the chapter on incest, one survivor writes a lengthy account of her six years of being raped by her father, and how he coerced her and controlled the family. Through her insights, we begin to see and feel what the incest survivor is up against, and to learn strategies for surviving this hellish experience. In the chapter on rape, a survivor writes about how she had been unable to trust boys or men, or to connect in a romantic relationship, until she began to speak out. What we learn from all these girls is that help is out there, that healing is possible, and that sexual abuse is never a girl's fault.

An organization called Generation Five was founded in 1997 with a mission to end the sexual abuse of children within five generations. This book is a part of that work. The more that girls are able to speak out and reach out, the more other girls will be encouraged to do the same. The less taboo the subject becomes, the more possible it will be to make changes— to public awareness, to the law and public policy, to the options for girls living with abusers or would-be abusers. You may not have been able to stop the abuse that happened to you, but you can start getting your life back together now and reach out to other girls. Together, eventually, we will make it impossible for men to get away with taking out their own rage or anger or fear or despair on women and girls through sexual violence.

If you are no longer being abused, this book will offer you perspective and healing; if you are currently living at home and being molested by a relative, it will provide you with critical emotional support and resources, even if you are not able to get away. And if you are just beginning to remember abuse that happened when you were younger, this book will help you find the strength and the right people to talk to so that you can start to heal.

We know that many girls who are abused end up taking detours in their lives—getting into drugs, sex, self-harm, or eating disorders. They often feel that the abuse is their destiny, the map of their lives. But I have worked with these girls, and I can tell you that every girl can heal from sexual abuse. My hope is that, by shedding some light on the problem, I can help you turn away from some of the darker choices other abused girls have made.

There is Help

If you are looking for urgent or ongoing support, please turn to the Resource Center at the back of this book for help. There you will find hotline numbers, websites, and counseling centers located throughout the country. The Resource Center also directs readers to my website, www.girlthrive.com, where additional resources, a chat room, a Q & A, and letters from young women can be found.

Together, we will be like artists building a beautiful mosaic: All the tiles we need to rebuild your soul, with its many nuances and imperfections and exquisite colorful complexities, are here. We just need to put them in their right places.

Into the Light

Girls and women are brilliant at surviving and at doing very deep psychological work to heal their own trauma. Whether through counseling, poetry, songwriting, art, or writing stories, or through telling a friend, a therapist, a parent, a school counselor, or a volunteer at an abuse hotline, the most important thing you can do is simply *tell someone,* because telling is the beginning of healing.

The girls whose stories fill this book heroically overcame shame and guilt and the tremendous burden of secrecy. It all began with telling someone. All they needed was a safe place and the permission to let out their secret. As I see it, my role and the role of this book is to provide that safe environment for other abuse survivors, as well as to enlighten those who have not been through the experience, but who care about these girls—be it a parent or a loved one, a counselor or an educator. If you are not a survivor, you will witness just how resilient the human spirit really is. If you *are* a survivor, you will be able to take comfort in the fact that you are not alone. And if you have just begun to process your experience, this book can help you make your way through the dark maze of feelings you have been holding inside. Together, we will find the light.

As one eighteen-year-old incest survivor wrote, "Out of all the piles of dirt, garbage, and shit we have been handed, we can grow a patch of daisies."

PART ONE
WHAT IS IN PANDORA'S BOX?
SEXUAL ABUSE AND HOW IT AFFECTS US

Chapter 1

Ask Dr. Patti
Answers to Girls' Questions about Sexual Abuse

Through the years, girls have asked me hundreds of questions about the many confusing feelings, statistics, and terms surrounding sexual abuse. I'm sure you have some questions, too, so I thought it would be helpful to share some of the questions, comments, and concerns I'm asked most frequently—and my responses—to help clear up some of the most common misunderstandings surrounding sexual abuse, and to direct you to the chapters that might be most helpful to you.

> Dear Dr. Patti,
>
> I keep hearing that sexual abuse is really widespread. I have never been sexually abused, and I don't have any friends who have been. Is it possible that the statistics are wrong?
>
> –Wondering

Dear Wondering,

Sadly, it's possible that you *do* know someone who has been or is being abused, but you just don't know it. Because of the stigma and the shame surrounding sexual abuse, many girls have trouble telling anyone about it, and that means, if anything, that the statistics you've heard are probably too low, not too high. The latest information I have (from a 1997 Commonwealth Fund study) is that one out of four American girls will experience some sort of sexual abuse by age sixteen—everything from a single incident where someone touched a girl's breasts without her permission to a ten-year experience of being raped nearly every day by a relative. These statistics apply across all economic and ethnic lines.

Dear Dr. Patti,

When I was ten years old, my uncle put his hand under my shirt and touched my chest. I got him to stop. He also rubbed up against me and tried to hold me to him. He lived far away, and I never saw him again. I never told anyone. Was I sexually abused? What exactly is sexual abuse?

—Concerned

Dear Concerned,

First, let me say that I'm very glad you do not have to deal with this uncle anymore. I'm sad to say that what you experienced was abuse. Even one inappropriate, unwanted touch is abuse. Generally, any unwanted sexual encounter constitutes abuse. The reason it's important to acknowledge that it was abuse is that otherwise it can eat away at you or make you feel ongoing conflicts about yourself and your sexuality. It's important to know that it was abuse so you are clear that it was not your fault.

There is non-touching sexual abuse and touching sexual abuse. Here's a list of some of the more common forms of both:

Touching Sexual Abuse

❁ having any of your private parts touched

❁ being fondled

❁ being penetrated genitally through sodomy or intercourse

❁ being asked to sit on the lap of an adult and having the adult rub their genitals against your skin

❖ having an adult rub against you or touch you in any way that makes you uncomfortable and refusing to stop when asked to

❖ having to watch an adult masturbate

Non-Touching Sexual Abuse

❖ being asked to view pornographic materials

❖ having pictures taken of you in sexual poses

❖ being spoken to with sexual intonation (i.e., "you look like a slut," "you must be screwing around," "look at your breasts; they look really firm")

❖ being walked in on repeatedly in the bathroom or your bedroom

❖ having an adult leave the bathroom door open repeatedly when they are inside

❖ being asked by an adult if they can check out your breasts and genitals

❖ being forced into conversations about sex

Dear Dr. Patti,

My uncle molested me and several of my cousins for years until one day my cousin (his daughter) couldn't take it anymore and told her mom. There was this big court case, and he actually went to jail for a short time because I told, and then five other cousins came forward, too. All of us had been molested by him before we were even teenagers. When he was arrested, he said, "I just couldn't help myself." What is a pedophile, and what makes someone a pedophile or a child molester?

–Confused and Hurt

Dear Confused,

First of all, there is no consensus on what makes a child

molester. There is a variety of opinions. What we do know is that these are men who seek out children. Some are homosexuals and seek out only boys. In our book we are looking specifically at men who sexually abuse girls. Many men who abuse children were abused in some way when they were younger. People who work with pedophiles tell us that these men may have felt they could not express themselves, that they felt they had no power except their power over someone much smaller. Sexual abuse is about sexual gratification, but it is also very much about power and manipulation.

Pedophilia is described as a condition of having deep sexual urges for children, but many, many pedophiles have sexual relations with adults, too. A father or uncle who abuses a daughter may still be having sex with his wife, for example.

In her book *Sleeping with a Stranger,* Patricia Wiklund describes sexual molesters as men who feel repressed and inadequate. They are morally and sexually indiscriminate. They have no conscience. I often find that molesters want us to feel sorry for them. That certainly seems to have been the case with your uncle when he whined that he couldn't help himself. What you need to remember is that it is never the survivor's fault.

Dear Dr. Patti,

I moved here from Trinidad when I was five years old. Many of my relatives still live in Trinidad and often come to visit in the summertime. The summer that I was nine years old, one of my visiting cousins started molesting me. He was sixteen when it started, and each summer he would do more stuff to me. He was always very nice to me, and I kind of liked the attention, but then he would make me touch his genitals and masturbate him. I was very confused. In a way it excited me, but it also scared me and made me feel weird.

He never penetrated me, but he performed oral sex on me and he made me perform oral sex on him. The oral sex made me gag, and sometimes I even vomited after. He was a very loved family member, and I never told anyone. It stopped the summer I turned fourteen; my cousin was in college by then and had stopped coming to the States. I am now nineteen and having a hard time sexually. I find myself turned off by sex and scared. Is this normal? Was I sexually abused? Was it incest? Is something wrong with me because it felt good to me sometimes?

–Confused and Scared

Dear Confused and Scared,

Yes, you were most definitely abused, and yes, it was incest. Any sexual contact between family members (or any adult figure you consider a family member) is incest. Your cousin knew better than to molest a nine-year-old girl. Girls who are being abused often get really confused when their bodies respond positively, but our bodies are stimulated by touch, and the fact that you liked this cousin would probably only add to that.

There is absolutely nothing wrong with you! As you will learn throughout the book, our bodies sometimes respond to touch and genital stimulation. It does not mean that you wanted sex when you were nine.

I don't know all the details of your family, but I'm assuming you didn't feel safe telling a parent. I understand. Often girls are afraid that if they tell a parent they will be blamed. Many girls also tell me that they are afraid of sex after any form of sexual abuse. They don't know whom or what to trust. Remember, it's okay to just explore romance at your age. Most girls go on to have good, healthy sexual relationships after abuse, but it can take some time.

You do not have to have sex with someone you are dating. You are in charge, and you can set the pace. If you do start dating, you can tell the guy you want to go very slowly.

If you have a trusted friend or adult you can speak to about what happened with your cousin, I encourage you to do so. You may also want to call the RAINN hotline or try some counseling. The more you talk about it, the better you'll feel. See Chapter 7 for more about sexual abuse by brothers, uncles, cousins, and stepfathers.

Dear Dr. Patti,

I am seventeen years old and go to high school in suburban Chicago. I have been dating my boyfriend for the past five months. I am a virgin and want to stay that way for now, but we just began to have oral sex. I did not like going down on him very much, but I agreed to do it a couple of times. Last week we were at his house, and we both were drinking. I think he was a bit drunk, and while I was giving him head, I started gagging. I stopped, and he was very upset and begged me to "finish what I started." I said no, and he pushed my head down forcefully. I felt like I couldn't breathe. He forced me to make him ejaculate. I was shocked. I never knew he was like that. I felt so vulnerable at the time; it was horrible. I felt like I was a toy and he could do anything he wanted with me.

I thought he loved me. I guess I was wrong. I hate loving somebody who doesn't really love me back. I could not seem to get him out of my mind and I chalked it up to his being drunk. Even though he did this to me and did not apologize, I went out with him again. The next time we were alone, he did the same thing, but this time I tried to fight and pull my mouth off his penis. He pushed my head so hard, I could not move or breathe. He would not let go of my head and shoulders to the point where I started gagging and actually vomited. I felt a mixture of disgust and embarrassment. He threw me off of him in disgust. We broke up after this last incident, and I feel really gross about what happened. Did I get sexually abused? Is this date rape even though he did not force intercourse on me?

–*Nauseous and Disappointed*

Dear Nauseous and Disappointed,

First of all, let me say how sorry I am about what happened with this boyfriend. Many girls talk about feeling nauseous performing oral sex on guys. There is a lot of pressure out there these days for girls to perform oral sex. No girl needs to agree to this if she does not want to. I should add that if you do not use a condom during oral sex, you are susceptible to sexually transmitted diseases. You should probably see a doctor to be sure you're okay.

Even though he did not penetrate you, I and many other psychologists would define forced oral sex as rape; in your case, date rape. Not all guys you date, of course, will do this.

Date rape, by the way, refers to any time you are forced to have sex with someone you are with on a date or that you ended up with at a given time by choice. Acquaintance rape is when you are raped by someone you know only slightly but were with voluntarily. According to an extensive study by the Pennsylvania Coalition Against Rape in 2002, 90 percent of both date and acquaintance rape involves alcohol. For more information, see Chapter 10.

Dear Dr. Patti,

I am in college, and one of my professors has made some comments to me and some of my friends that have made us kind of uncomfortable. He said we are pretty. He seems to stare at us. He told me not to worry about my grade because I am so attractive. Are we being sexually abused or sexually harassed? What's the difference?

–College Blues

Dear College Blues,

While what you are experiencing is sexual harassment, it could also be called non-touching sexual abuse. Sexual harassment is the generally accepted legal term, but it is really a form of non-touching sexual abuse. For example, if you are walking down the hallway in school or on the street and some man or boy calls out something like, "Hey, babe, you look sexy! Nice ass! Let's screw!" or "Can I have some!" it may not result in a physical assault, but it can certainly feel scary if you are alone, and it can even bring up some of the same bad feelings that you'd have in an ongoing abusive relationship. I would suggest that you and your friends keep a record of these comments and then go to the dean and file a complaint. His comments could turn into abuse, and in any case, he has no right to make you feel uncomfortable.

There is a very fine line between sexual harassment and sexual abuse. You may read many different definitions of these two terms. Usually abuse involves some sort of physical violation, but it is more complicated than that. If I have a client who tells me that during her entire adolescence her father never touched her but looked at her in a sexual way all the time, walked around naked in the house, left out pornographic materials, and called her a slut when she went out with her boyfriend, I would have to say she was sexually abused. Thus abuse really does encompass those situations in which sexual statements are so constant that they create a climate of abuse.

Sexual abuse refers to being violated sexually. If the perpetrator never touches you, but you feel totally violated by his words and looks and lack of boundaries, you may have the same feelings as a girl who has been violated through touch, so there's not always that much difference in the end. Quite often, too, verbal sexual violation accompanies physical violation. For more information, see Chapter 8.

Dear Dr. Patti,

Is sexual abuse happening more now than in earlier times, or are we just hearing about it more?

–Generation X

Dear Generation X,

Only in the past few decades have people been able to compile any reliable statistics on sexual abuse, because before that, the whole subject was so taboo that very few people ever reported or talked about it. However, over the past ten years or so, researchers have consistently found that one out of four girls in the United States will experience some form of sexual abuse—from invasive sexual touching to rape—by the time she is sixteen. Psychiatrist Alice Miller wrote extensively about the abuse of all children, particularly girls, going back to the nineteenth century (see Bibliography), and recent work has suggested that Freud's "seduction theory" was a cover-up for the rampant sexual abuse of young girls (see Introduction and Bibliography). Unfortunately, we have no reason to think that sexual abuse hasn't been happening for centuries.

Dear Dr. Patti,

I feel trapped in a catch-22. Obviously, if it were not for my father, I would not be here. But to be genetically connected to a monster like him—he raped me for most of my childhood—scares me so much. I am afraid that I will end up hurting children, too. I am very protective around kids, but the truth is, I am afraid to babysit because I think I will do something weird. Is pedophilia genetic? I can't even imagine ever hurting anyone, especially a child, but am I destined somehow to be like him?

–*Trapped by My Genetics*

Dear Trapped,

No, no, and no! You do not have any genetic predisposition to being a child molester. I can assure you that there are almost no reported cases of female sexual-abuse survivors ever molesting anyone. You do not have any genes that will turn you into a pedophile. I suggest that you take on some babysitting to prove to yourself that you will be fine with kids. I trust you. Please trust yourself. If you are very nervous about this, you can think about the way you are with children. If anything, I have found incest survivors to be particularly protective of small children. For more information, see Chapter 6.

Dear Dr. Patti,

I saw this movie once where a woman suddenly remembered her father molesting her when she was a girl, but when she had her court case, they said she made it up. They called it "False Memory Syndrome." Do girls make up sexual abuse? What exactly is False Memory Syndrome, and when did this all come about?

–Confused

Dear Confused,

False Memory Syndrome, as you suggest, refers to stories that are supposedly "made up" by suggestible patients under hypnosis. The "syndrome" was named in 1992 by clinicians at the University of Pennsylvania and Johns Hopkins University in response to charges and lawsuits having to do with allegations of childhood sexual abuse ten, twenty, fifty years after it had happened. They claimed that memories can too easily get distorted over time, and that there simply wasn't good evidence to support the stories of thousands of women who were coming forward with memories of past sexual abuse. In all cases of sexual abuse, evidence is difficult to gather, unless a woman or girl actually has a semen sample from inside her own vagina. Let me say this: Children don't usually lie, and I have never met a girl or a woman who has made up a sexual-abuse experience. Sometimes, if abuse happened before a baby knew how to talk, the memory will be stored in the form of feelings, and it can be trickier to reconstruct what happened, but that isn't the same as a lie. (It is interesting to note that the False Memory Syndrome Foundation was created by two parents, Pamela and Peter Freyd, who were charged with sexual abuse by their own daughter.)

Of course, there are exceptions to every rule, and there have undoubtedly been some cases where a child or young woman was misled by an incompetent therapist into believing she was abused. But the evidence suggests that this is very, very rare. The vast majority of girls well know the difference between reality and fantasy. For more information, see Chapter 5.

Dear Dr. Patti,

When I went to see a therapist about my abuse, she wanted me to go under hypnosis. I was really frightened. She had me close my eyes and asked me to do what she told me. I couldn't relax because my father always had me close my eyes before he would molest me. Then she wanted me to do EMDR [Eye Movement Desensitization and Reprogramming, another therapeutic technique], and that scared me, too. I have never been back to a therapist since. Is hypnosis really necessary for therapy?

–Eyes Wide Open

Dear Eyes Wide Open,

Some people claim that long-repressed memories are best recovered under hypnosis, and professionals do undergo very specific training to become hypnotherapists. However, it is not proven as a "cure" for repressed memories, and in the wrong hands, it can certainly be misleading and harmful. In order for hypnosis to work, the person being hypnotized must trust the hypnotherapist enough to give up control to her, which makes it a complicated and controversial technique for sexual-abuse survivors.

Proponents of hypnosis claim that it can open up and clarify memories that were otherwise vague. Opponents claim that thoughts and memories can be "planted" by suggestion. Many sexual-abuse survivors have told me how frightening it is to undergo hypnosis and give trust over to someone else. In any case, hypnosis is generally not recommended for adolescents because their memories are usually pretty sharp.

EMDR is another therapeutic technique that is based on the idea that hidden memories can be uncovered. It was developed in the late 1980s based on the theory that because disturbing memories are stored in the brain, they can be "replaced" by new memories, which are uncovered by thinking about the disturbing event while also focusing on something pleasing. In other words, the memories can be reconfigured. Some people claim great results with EMDR, and it has the added benefit of working with your eyes open.

Both hypnosis and EMDR are best used in conjunction with psychotherapy. In my experience, longer-term psychotherapy is the most curative, because you are able to take time to establish trust with the therapist, which is very important when trying to heal from something as traumatic as sexual abuse. For more information, see Chapter 11.

Dear Dr. Patti,

A few days ago I reported my father to the police for sexually abusing me. My whole family has now broken up. I haven't eaten in two days, and I cannot get out of bed. I am lonely and miserable, and on top of it, I feel guilty. My mother says I am seriously depressed and is threatening to make me go to a psych hospital.

–Despondent

Dear Despondent,

What you did takes great courage, and the feelings you are having are not only normal but very, very healthy. You are finally allowing yourself to feel the feelings you couldn't allow yourself to feel at the time of the abuse so you could get through it. You are allowing your body to break down under the weight of what happened. Please tell your mother not to be afraid of these feelings and encourage her to get some counseling so she can understand what to expect during this time. In fact, most states courts will mandate therapy for both the child and the mother in incest cases. The father will also receive treatment, as well as punishment.

Depression lasts at least a few weeks and involves too much or too little sleep and/or eating, loss of interest in your usual activities, and feelings of hopelessness. If you continue to sleep all the time and feel miserable, you may be headed toward a depression, and by all means, I'd urge you to get some professional help (with a counselor or therapist or guidance counselor) to clarify and get a handle on your feelings. But for now, you and your mother should understand that it's healthy and normal to feel scared and depressed after reporting sexual abuse. You might try to find a support group for you and your mom (see our Resource Center section for ideas). Also, show your mom this book. Try to reassure her that you are all right, and that you need her, not a psych hospital, right now.

As far as guilt goes, if your father abused you, you have nothing to feel guilty about. He is the one who is guilty. For more information, see Chapters 3, 6, and 7.

Dear Dr. Patti,

I have reported my father for incest. I am sixteen now, and he molested me starting when I was twelve. He was given eight months in prison and then ordered to go to therapy for two years. My mother wants our family back together again, and my father says with treatment he won't touch me again. I am scared and want to go and live with my very supportive aunt. My mother says I can. Should I? Do you think my father is "cured"? Are child molesters ever "cured"?

–Wanting Out

Dear Wanting Out,

First of all, I agree with you. I think you should move in with your aunt.

This is really a two-part question, and first I will address the moving-out part. There are different schools of thought about this. Some therapists believe that it is usually best to keep families together, and that after treatment, most abusers can work things out with their families. I belong to the opposite school. I believe that if a father or stepfather molests his daughter, the mother must make it her first priority to protect and support her daughter and should never take him back. This is an unforgivable abuse. The daughter is not the guilty party and should not be made to live with a man who abused her. I think that therapy can be necessary for mother and daughter, but I believe that both should be encouraged to keep away from the molester. Your mother pushing you to support the reenty of your father into the family may just make you feel violated all over again. If your aunt says it's okay to live with her, I think you should do it, and not put yourself further in emotional harm's way.

My colleague Kay Jackson, who has worked with pedophiles for twenty years, has seen some families actually come back together with some success. But Dr. Jackson also says that pedophilia is not "curable," per se. She says that it lasts forever, but that some men can learn to control it. It has been her experience that only through severe punishment (i.e., jail time) and intensive therapy can some men rehabilitate. But you shouldn't have to be the guinea pig. Your only responsibility is to care for yourself. For more information, see Chapters 3 and 6.

Dear Dr. Patti,

I have seen movies where women have multiple personalities. In the movies they are usually incest survivors. Is this just in the movies? I am an incest survivor, and sometimes I feel like I change my personality a lot. I can be pretty moody. My friend tells me I may have Multiple Personality Disorder. Do all incest and sex-abuse survivors have it?

–More Than One Me?

Dear More Than One?,

No, not all incest survivors develop Multiple Personality Disorder (MPD). MPD is a clinical diagnosis defined as a "splitting" of a personality into two or more separate personalities to protect a person from various memories. A person with MPD actually creates a second personality (or more) with its own complete (or near-complete) identity. Incest survivors who are suffering deeply will often develop another persona as a survival strategy—to withstand the abuse. Also, as you will see in later chapters, girls who are experiencing sexual abuse often develop elaborate fantasy worlds, but this shouldn't be confused with MPD. As a matter of fact, I see these fantasy worlds as very healing for girls. Girls have an amazing ability to protect themselves and survive the unspeakable. For more information, see Chapter 5.

Dear Dr. Patti,

I am an incest survivor. The problem I have is that I am so unaware of my body. When I fall, I don't feel pain. When my friends hug me, I barely feel their hugs, and, even worse, when my boyfriend kisses me, I don't feel any excitement. I want to feel connected to my body, but when I was molested I went numb; I felt as if I was floating out of my body. Will I ever have feelings again?

–Uncomfortably Numb

Dear Numb,

The sensation of floating you describe is often reported by incest survivors. The clinical term for it is disassociation, which is defined as removing oneself from a situation as a way to avoid the physical contact. You floated out of your body and became numb to protect yourself. You floated to live through the abuse.

It will take time, but you will be able to feel again. As time goes on and you are away from the perpetrator of your abuse, you will begin to trust again. It may begin in nonsexual ways, with friends hugging you. You might want to make an effort to give a close friend a hug and try to be aware of how you feel. The fact that you are letting your boyfriend get close is a good sign. Some girls say that when they tell their boyfriends about their abuse, it helps them to physically feel again. If you would be comfortable doing that, you might want to broach the subject and see how it goes. For more information, see Chapters 5 and 6.

Dear Dr. Patti,

After 9/11, I heard a lot about Post-Traumatic Stress Disorder. Is this disorder something that happens with sexual abuse, too?

—*Stressed*

Dear Stressed,

Yes, Post-Traumatic Stress Disorder, or PTSD, is a commonly accepted diagnosis for individuals who have experienced sexual abuse, the trauma of war, or serious tragedy. It is often the case that people are able to survive trauma only by becoming numb to their feelings about the trauma. For example, during a war soldiers can't allow themselves to feel their feelings of terror, or they would probably fall apart. In very much the same way, a sexual-abuse survivor (particularly one who is abused repeatedly) cannot afford to stop and feel the terror and trauma, or she could not withstand the abuse.

After the trauma, the survivor may be haunted with recurrent and intrusive memories of the trauma, recurrent dreams of the trauma, fear that the trauma will recur because of a stimulation in the environment (also referred to as a "trigger"), sleep disturbance or hypersleep (too much sleep), depression, panic attacks, or trouble concentrating. These are all symptoms of PTSD. If you think you may be suffering from PTSD, I urge you to see a professional.

Dear Dr. Patti,

I think my cousin may be getting abused by her dad. She denies it, but she's suddenly been very depressed and doesn't want to go out. She says her dad wants her home most of the time, which seems pretty strange to me. Meanwhile, her dad's been acting really weird and possessive around her. He's always had a creepy vibe around girls anyway. How can I tell if he's abusing her?

–*Concerned Cousin*

Dear Concerned,

While none of the following traits in and of themselves are "evidence" of abuse, there are some common survivor's traits to look out for:

* low self-esteem

* promiscuity

* fear of sex

* fear of intimacy

* large blocks of memory loss

* nightmares

* anxiety attacks

* mistrusting men

* poor relationship with mother

* perfectionism

* repulsion from certain "triggers," i.e., a gesture, a touch, a smell, a voice, or anything that might bring up memories of the molestation

* poor body image

If you really think your cousin is being abused, find someone you can trust to talk with—perhaps your mother or an older sister or a counselor. You can also call the RAINN hotline at 1 (800) 656-HOPE (800-656-4673) and get some advice. If you can locate a counseling center nearby (RAINN can help), you could ask your cousin if she is being abused and then let her know that you are willing to go with her to counseling if she wishes. We address all of the above survivor traits throughout the book.

Dear Dr. Patti,

I am eighteen years old and a senior in high school. I was born here, but my parents were born in Russia. They have brought over many family members through the years. My uncle, who came here about five years ago, started molesting me when I was fourteen. I basically put up with it, but when he started bothering my younger sister, I decided I had to do something. So I told my mother. Then I went to school and told my school counselor. The police came and arrested my uncle.

My mother threw me out of the house and won't let me come back until I go to the police and tell them that I lied. I am so scared. I'm about to graduate from high school. What should I do? Was I wrong to tell?

–Made to Lie

Dear Made to Lie,

First of all, telling is almost always frightening, and sometimes it may not feel like telling is the right thing to do, even when it is, because it is so scary. For girls from cultures that view girls as less important than boys, or cultures where the mother is less powerful than the father, deciding not to tell her family might be the best thing a girl can do to take care of herself.

Please go back to your school counselor and ask for help. Find a trusted friend to stay with. The fact that you broke open the abuse may have saved your sister (in many incest situations, a girl doesn't tell until a younger sibling or cousin is being threatened, too). If you have no one to turn to, please see our Resource Center for guidance; see also Chapters 7, 12, and 13.

Dear Dr. Patti,

My uncle molested me five years ago. When I told my counselor at school recently, he told me that he had to report it because he didn't want the "statute of limitations" to run out. He was also worried, he said, because my uncle has two daughters under the age of fifteen.

It turned out that my uncle was arrested, and my mother and father were really grateful to me for telling, but I'm really confused about the laws about reporting and everything. Can you explain?

–*Confused about the Law*

Dear Confused about the Law,

Dealing with reporting and the courts can be very confusing, and it's true that the laws vary from state to state. But there is always someone in the police department who works with victims services. The term "statute of limitations" refers to a time limit on when a person can be prosecuted for crimes he or she allegedly committed. Please see our Resource Center for more information.

Dear Dr. Patti,

I'm in college, and a few weeks ago, my friend came over to my house crying. She had just been raped by her boyfriend, who was visiting from out of town. I didn't know what to do for her. She told me she just wanted to take a long shower to wash off all she was feeling. She took a shower, and then I made her some hot chocolate, and she went home. A couple of weeks later, she asked me to come with her to the police to report the rape. The police told us we had no evidence and it would be really difficult to prosecute. My friend is despondent. When should a rape be reported?

—Trying to Be a Good Friend

Dear Trying,

Your friend is lucky to have you in her life. You did the best you could for her. Unfortunately, what the police told you is true. It's almost impossible to prosecute a rape case without physical evidence, and as soon as your friend showered, she effectively destroyed what evidence there was.

It's very important to first go to a hospital and do what's called a "rape kit." This medical exam takes a tissue and fluid sample from the vagina, checks for injury, STDs, and pregnancy, and administers RU-486 to prevent pregnancy, where possible. The police will also come to the hospital to make a report. Please see Chapter 10 for more about what to do following a date rape.

Dear Dr. Patti,

I am gay, and I was at a club with some friends. I was dancing all night with this girl I was attracted to. After we left the club we went to her apartment. We had both been drinking, and we started fooling around. I only wanted to kiss and she wanted more. She became violent and pulled off my shirt and pants and forced her fingers inside my vagina. I tried to push her off but could not. I finally got away. Was I date-raped?

—Female Raped?

Dear Female Raped?

I'm so sorry this happened to you. Yes, you were date-raped. It may not be considered rape by law, but it is just as emotionally damaging. Whether it's done by a boy/man or a girl/woman, whether it's "just" oral sex or full-on penetration, whenever force is used, it's rape.

Dear Dr. Patti,

A female friend and I explored each other's bodies when we were about six years old. We played doctor and touched each other all over. We didn't hurt each other or anything, just explored. I don't feel really weird about it, but I am wondering if we sexually abused each other. I really like guys and don't think I'm gay, but why did we do this that one time?

–Child's Play

Dear Child's Play,

Sounds like you and your friend were indulging in normal curiosity. If you had been hurt by each other, felt coerced, did it multiple times, or felt a real drive to touch your friend's genitals and have your genitals touched; or if a same-age playmate, cousin, or sibling tried to force a toy or finger into your vagina or anus, that could certainly qualify as abuse. But many children explore once or twice, and that's perfectly healthy.

Children usually know, intuitively, the qualitative difference between exploratory fun play that includes some touching and being violated.

Dear Dr. Patti,

This feels like a stupid question, but it is something that haunts me. I was sexually abused by my father from the ages of nine through thirteen, until he died. Now I am eighteen, and I am in love for the first time. When my boyfriend and I made love, I told him I was a virgin. I am not ready to speak about my abuse, and truly, I feel like a virgin, even though my father penetrated me. Could I still be considered a virgin?

–Hoping

Dear Hoping,

I consider you a virgin. I have spoken to hundreds of girls who feel exactly the way you do. They were penetrated by their molesters, and they would never have lost their virginity to them by choice. Giving yourself sexually to your boyfriend is the first time you chose to do it. Others may disagree, but in my opinion, you are a virgin.

Dear Dr. Patti,

How can families let sexual abuse happen? Don't parents want to protect their children?

–Perplexed

Dear Perplexed,

Now there's a question that deserves a whole chapter. Read on. . . .

Chapter 2

Crossing Over

Girlhood to Womanhood

"One minute I'm up, the next I'm down

One minute I'm here, the next I'm there

My feelings seem real, but then they don't

At times things make sense, but then again they don't

One minute I'm happy, the next I'm sad

Where will I be? Where can I be?

Will you love me if I want your love?

Will you love me even if at first I turn away?"

The teenage girl who wrote this poem was expressing all the normal ups and downs of adolescence. Most sexual abuse takes place during this very vulnerable time in a girl's life—between the ages of around eleven and fifteen. This is the time of your first period, your first budding sexual feelings. Your body is undergoing extraordinary changes. Perhaps this is when you have your first crush, and maybe you grow six inches. And you are vulnerable to abuse because you are in such transition and don't yet know how to handle your developing body, or all these new expectations of how you should look and act and be, not to mention your own burgeoning sexual feelings. All sexual abuse is about being pushed beyond your own natural boundaries, but at twelve or thirteen or fifteen, girls usually don't even know what their own boundaries are. It's all so confusing.

In this chapter, we'll get into the psyche of the young teenage girl. We'll look at the cultural, physical, emotional, sexual, and psychological changes and pressures on adolescent girls, so that when we hear from the sex-abuse survivors later in this book, and when you look at your own life, you will have a full perspective on all that goes on during this time of great change.

Until around nine or ten years of age, many girls are still supportive of one another. They still communicate openly with each other about their feelings and struggles. They still trust their gut instincts. They go for the ball in soccer with a vengeance; they smack the tennis ball and don't worry if their skirt flies up. They know whom they like and whom they dislike and are not afraid to go after things they want. (True, they may still play with Barbies, but at least Barbie is just a doll.)

But as their bodies start to develop, things change. As their breasts grow, it becomes more and more difficult to run fast. It's more challenging to swim when they have their period. It becomes harder for them to choose what they "want." Gender roles, hormonal changes, and cultural expectations all collide as girls try to figure out how to fit in. Because of the male-dominated culture they live in, they begin to distrust their instincts; they begin to doubt themselves and give a lot of weight to what their peer group thinks.

Girls look to their friends for guidance and social footing. At the same time, adolescent girls may start to feel intense competition with one another as they jockey for social position, and they can become downright vicious as they compete in a male-dominated culture. That kind of viciousness just doesn't happen among younger girls.

It's hard being an adolescent girl. Add any other stresses—divorcing parents, the death of a close friend or relative, moving and starting a new school, breaking out with acne—and you can end up feeling very helpless and alone, and much more vulnerable to social pressures.

Adolescent girls are desperate to fit in, but they also realize that there's more at stake than ever. Because of the societal pressure to act and look in particular ways, i.e., demure and sexy, many girls find it more difficult to speak their minds. Depending on their cultural background and peer group, they may start to edit themselves in different ways in an effort to fit in.

In her research, psychologist Lyn Mikel Brown recently found that girls like many of you, girls from middle-class and affluent homes, have a much more difficult time expressing their anger than girls of lower income and less privilege. These girls are raised to be good, compliant, and successful. Invisible girls often have to overcome many years of conditioning to find their power and their voices.

Around this time, girls also start needing greater independence from their parents. They'll start to push their parents away, even though they still need them—sometimes desperately. That push/pull is all part of the transition from girlhood to womanhood, from childhood to adulthood.

Adolescent girls begin to suffer, often acutely, if not consciously, from the effects of sexism and male domination, all of which may have seemed irrelevant when they were younger. They can sense that their options in the world are shrinking. People are now more interested in how they look and how they interact socially than in their achievements. They know that they are being increasingly defined by their sex appeal, even if they don't feel sexy at all, and often don't know how to handle all the sexual attention.

Consider how all females are socialized to take on blame and responsibility for everything that happens at the interpersonal level. Girls who have been molested are no different. You often feel tremendous guilt and shame; you often feel it's somehow your fault. Let us say it again: It *never* is.

And our culture is pushing girls earlier and earlier to be "sexy." This is reinforced constantly by music videos. In one of her videos, "Baby One More Time," Britney Spears was made up to look like a young schoolgirl as she strutted around in her little school uniform. The "Lolita" story gives us perfect evidence of the disparity between what a young girl may have been feeling and how her actions are interpreted by older men. I'll never forget hearing a radio interview with Adrian Lyne, the director of the 1997 remake of the film *Lolita*, in which he talked about the young teenage girl he chose for the title role. Apparently she was chewing gum when she came in for her screen test, and when it was time for her to perform she took the gum from her mouth and stuck it to her leg so she could read the script. We can guess that she did this as the most efficient way to get rid of the gum while preserving it to chew later on. Well, that's not what this sixty-something man saw. He said it was one of the most "sensuous" gestures he had ever seen, and that he knew instantly that she would get the part. This is the way teen girls are seen in our sexist culture—as a handy package of "innocent" and "seducer" rolled into one.

No wonder girls can begin to distrust their instincts and act in counterintuitive ways. Girls may know what they are feeling, but they also feel an intense pressure, from inside and out, to go against their feelings and conform to societal pressures and messages. They're usually dealing with intense school pressure and are busy negotiating greater independence from their parents, and at the same time, they are being bombarded with advertisements and articles and imagery that is constantly telling them how to be sexier. Advertisers, TV sitcoms, magazines, music videos . . . the whole world is telling them it's great to become a woman, it's great to be sexy and attractive, and it's great to have sex.

One of my clients who was an incest survivor wrote at twenty:

"No one saw all the pain and suffering locked inside me when I was thirteen; no one took me aside and told me I would be all right. I wish I could go back and look at that girl, because I think I would tell her to stop giving herself away, to keep some part of her soul for her own, to tell the truth everywhere and always. To stay out of the myths and conspiracies and the 'protection' of the family. I would hold her and tell her to live for herself, and to get the hell away from the crazy people."

All this said, as difficult as adolescence can be, it can also be a time of wonderment. Many girls fall in love for the first time before they are eighteen, and many girls have loving, beautiful relationships with boyfriends or girlfriends. And even if you are an abuse survivor or come from a family with lots of troubles, you too can find this comfort and love once you leave your abuse behind you.

Chapter 3

Troubled Families

That incest survivor who wanted to go back and hold the thirteen-year-old girl who had been so damaged knew, at twenty, that her family was crazy to allow the abuse and not protect her. That's how sexual abuse happens. Innocent children need guidance and protection and don't receive it. In some fundamental way, all sexual abuse, with the exception of stranger rape, is about families failing their children. Girls would rather blame themselves, would rather hold their abuse inside, than go to their parents. They know that their parents would not believe them, would blame them, would fall apart if they knew. This is failure on a massive scale.

In the coming chapters, you will be meeting many girls whose parents failed them. Amber, whom you will meet in Chapter 9, had parents who may have loved her but were "old world" and not emotionally equipped to help her with the unhealthy sexual relationship she'd developed at camp with an older boy. Coral suffered incest at the hands of her biological father for six years, because she knew her mother, who turned out to also be an incest survivor, would not protect her. Sage's parents were too preoccupied to notice that anything was wrong. And on it goes. None of these girls had the kind of family support that makes a girl feel protected and cared for, loved and cherished.

It doesn't matter what kind of family you live in—one-parent, two-parent, grandparent, foster, or adoptive: When the adults you count on to protect you aren't there for you, you are more vulnerable to being abused, both inside and outside the four walls of home.

Of course, it's dangerous to make too many sweeping generalizations about families where abuse occurs. The point is simply this: If you were sexually abused and could not go to your family for support, you deserve to realize that your family failed you fundamentally. Your parents did not provide a safe atmosphere of support and protection for their children, which is a parent's first responsibility. It was not your fault. You were abused because no one was there to protect you or teach you the necessary skills to be safe.

Of course, some families do give abused girls the support they need, but those girls are not the invisible ones, the ones with the deep scars. If you were abused, even randomly by a stranger, and did not feel safe enough to run to your parents for protection, if you feel in any way that your parents would blame you for the abuse, not stand up for you, or not confront your abuser, it is important for you to understand that the problem lies with your family, not with you. You'll see this clearly when you read the other girls' stories.

Incest Families

"I was such a little girl then, and I knew it felt bad, and I knew it hurt, but my daddy said it was the right thing to do, our little se-cret. He said it would upset my mommy to know. My mom never asked why my daddy always needed to give me a bath, so I never told her. I would just sit there in the tub, numb, and listen to her footsteps as she walked by the closed door."

—A SEVENTEEN-YEAR-OLD INCEST SURVIVOR

I think it goes without saying that incest families are unhealthy and unsupportive families, if only because they don't protect their daughters. Men don't get away with incest when a strong, able mother is present. They just don't. Incest continues when girls know they wouldn't be safe telling. They know their mothers can't or won't protect them. Of course, sometimes these girls don't have a mother. But in the great majority of cases, the mother is present and simply can't cope with the reality of the abuse.

Many of our mothers were themselves sexually abused, either as children or as adults or both. These are women who learned to put up with whatever men dish out. They had to, and they've passed along that passivity and/or fear to their daughters. Because they were not able to heal from their own trauma, they often carry their damaged self-esteem, their addiction, and/or their mental illness into their roles as mothers. But you have a chance to do things differently.

One of my clients tells a remarkable story. When she finally told her mother and grandmother that her great-grandfather had molested her when she was a little girl, her grandmother said, "He molested me, too." And her mother said, "Me, too." But when my client tried to dig a little deeper, both women clammed up. Here were three generations of abuse survivors, and still they couldn't quite face up to the truth. You can break the cycle.

Emotionally Unsupportive Families

It's not just in incest families that families let their daughters down. I've worked with many girls whose families ignored their pleas for help after an experience of sexual abuse. I've had girls tell me of parents who blamed them after they spoke of being pushed too far by their boyfriends, called them sluts and whores, and accused them of "asking for it." In Chapter 7, "Too Close for Comfort," Sage talks about getting thrown out of the house at eighteen because she was "too much trouble." Often these girls are in a real bind, too. They might want to go on to college, but they're often on their own financially. Some are trapped in the catch-22 of being claimed as dependents on their parents' taxes—and thus unable to get financial aid—even though their parents are no longer supporting them.

Another way parents let down their daughters is by having no clear boundaries—not just emotional boundaries, but also physical ones. I consider certain actions that might not be incest, per se, to be incestuous. For example, I have heard many stories from girls whose fathers walked around naked or never shut the door when they were getting dressed or made suggestive comments to their daughters about their breasts or asses. Often, when these girls spoke up to protest their father's behavior, their families accused them of being prudish or repressed, and the girls developed real insecurities about their own rights to boundaries.

Fathers don't have to rape their daughters or do anything secretive to effectively violate and silence their daughters. Girls know when their feelings will not be respected. They also know when it's not safe to set their own terms within the family. Girls left voiceless like this are at much greater risk of being abused.

When we are small children, we depend on our parents for everything. Without them, we would be unprotected. Without them, we would be unclothed, unfed, uncared for. We begin in the world needing our parents for survival, and as life goes on, they are the ones we should be able to turn to for comfort and guidance.

But our families sometimes either give us poor guidance or do not guide us at all. I've worked with many girls whose parents simply couldn't cope, and so the kids had to take on the role of adults, with no one to protect them, as well as with girls from families in which kids have no voice at all; families in which the parents are too busy, too wrapped up in their own lives to notice; and families in which girls are made to feel ashamed of their sexuality. The list goes on.

The fact that so many families are able to betray their daughters is just another symptom of the way our culture perpetuates male domination. For all the gains women have made, girls still struggle to make their voices heard, to have power. And girls whose parents can't take proper care of them are left to float without a life preserver. They are made to fend for themselves and navigate their sexuality and emotions, and are more or less set up to be mistreated because they have not been taught how valuable they are as human beings.

During adolescence, girls are just beginning to seek full expression of themselves, and if that expression is blocked, girls tend to go either inward into depression or outward to unhealthy behaviors. This is why I believe so strongly that for girls who have been sexually abused, this is the time to talk about the emotions surrounding your sexual abuse, to expel all the difficult feelings about the abuse, and to begin to heal. You are still young enough to get rid of the emotional baggage of sexual abuse that might otherwise haunt you in adulthood. You are young enough to become whole, to become visible, to recover.

In a perfect world, of course, there would be no sexual abuse. Men and boys simply wouldn't cross the line, and if they ever tried, girls wouldn't be afraid to fight back or speak up. They would be able to count on support, and they'd know that they would be believed. But this isn't a perfect world, of course, so you'll need to find the people who will advocate for you and protect you and cherish you. Friends, aunts, cousins, teachers, counselors—these are the people who can be your anchor in the world when your family fails you.

As you read the stories in the following chapters, remember that you are here now because you are strong and capable and a survivor. Your family may not have been there to help you, but you did what it took to get through the experience of your abuse, and now you are ready to heal. You are ready to find and face your truth. You are ready to become visible.

Chapter 4

Finding Your Truth

Facing the Emotional Aftershocks and
the Beginning of Healing

"All at once the ghosts come back . . .

Slip-sliding at a pace unlike any other . . ."

—AN EIGHTEEN-YEAR-OLD INCEST SURVIVOR

On the website of the feminist punk band Le Tigre, one of the members of the band, Kathleen Hanna, talks about being a sex-abuse survivor. She cautions girls to be careful about whom they disclose their abuse to. One thing a lot of abuse survivors have in common is that they were not taught how to have good boundaries, and it's easy to wind up telling someone who isn't really all that safe. I think she's right. You want to be cautious about whom you tell. However, she also describes girls who tell as the links in the chain that will make the world a better place for everyone. I agree here, too. The more girls speak out and tell their stories, the more healing there will be, and the harder it will be for the culture to keep sexual abuse so invisible.

In fact, the basic premise of this book is that the best way to heal from sexual abuse is to talk about it, and that the best time to talk is now, while you are still young. From adolescence through your mid-twenties, you are most able to change and grow. You can heal the scars of your abuse the more you talk about it—now. Sexual abuse leaves wounds, but wounds heal, and if you can get to them now, they won't have time to grow deep roots and cause you lifelong suffering.

If you wait until you are in your thirties or later, problems stemming from childhood sexual abuse will almost always have grown those deep roots and be harder to deal with. Sexual abuse tries to rob women of their self-worth and self-esteem, and such untended wounds put women at greater risk for date rape and abusive marriages. That's one of the reasons it's so important to speak out now and start healing.

Finding Outlets for Your Feelings

"When I run the track at school, I am in a zone—a zone where there is no abuse and no rape."

—A SEVENTEEN-YEAR-OLD RAPE SURVIVOR

Often, before we can talk about the traumas that have happened to us, we have to find outlets for our feelings. Whether you realize it, you probably already have a number of such outlets. Maybe those long runs at the track are helping you get out your anger. Maybe singing those gorgeous and sad Gregorian chants have been giving you a channel for some deep pain; maybe drawing strong women with full bodies in drawing studio has been making your body feel healed. That's part of the genius of the body and mind: We are often self-healing without even realizing it.

Girls find many different ways of expressing their feelings about their sexual abuse. Some girls find writing to be the best way to get it out. I know an eighteen-year-old who filled three journals with drawings and writings about her incest. She said that every time she wrote or drew some of her feelings, she felt she let go of pieces of the pain. In our Resource Center, we have listed some zines where young incest survivors share their artwork and writing.

Whatever helps you get the feelings out—kickboxing, drawing, dancing, writing poetry—do it. I've heard girls describe how running gives them a visceral feeling of letting go of some of the tension in their rigid bodies. They are literally letting go of the inner shame and pain with every stride. Girls who dance several times a week talk about dancing the pain out of their bodies and souls.

※　　※　　※

Digging Deep

"Drumming is my mantra. I bang out all my anger."

—A NINETEEN-YEAR-OLD RAPE SURVIVOR

All of the above assumes, of course, that you have access to your feelings. Sometimes, especially if you are still living at home, it can be too dangerous to let yourself feel. You may still be living with your incestuous father or still go to school with the boys who gang-raped you or go to the church where the priest abused you. Often, when girls are living under the same roof with their abuser, they need to suppress their pain. It's a survival mechanism you may need until you move away from your abuser. But once you are ready to acknowledge that you were sexually violated, the healing can begin.

Triggers

"It feels like I try to calm the anger that erupts inside like a volcano as my mind blows like a hurricane."

—A NINETEEN-YEAR-OLD INCEST SURVIVOR

Some girls find that memories of their abuse experience come back with certain smells or sounds, such as when they hear a certain song on the radio or when they are touched in a certain way. These are called "triggers." One of my clients was molested in the bathtub, and anytime she tried to take a bath after that, it triggered memories of her molestation. Another client could not stand having her lover whisper to her during intimacy because her brother used to whisper and cover her mouth when he abused her.

All kinds of experiences can act as triggers—whether you like it or not, or expect it or not. It can happen when you're watching a movie or reading a book and you find yourself identifying with a character who was abused. Or it might happen when another girl starts telling you what happened to her and you suddenly realize, "Yes, that happened to me, too. What my brother/uncle/father/family friend did to me was rape. It was incest; it was sexual violation!"

Other girls talk about seasonal triggers. One girl I knew recounted how her father would molest her under the changing leaves of a tree in her backyard. Now, whenever the leaves change and she feels the brisk wind on her face, she remembers and feels ill. Another client remembers being gang-raped in the heat of summer. There are certain smells that come up in humidity that bring her right back to the scene in her mind.

Triggers are not controllable. But by recognizing what they are and when and why they occur, you can consciously re-map your emotions. My client who was molested in the bath, for instance, made the choice to take back the experience of bathing. She bought herself bath oils and candles and played soft, sweet music so she could relax into the soothing waters. It didn't work overnight, of course, but now she really enjoys a hot bath and no longer associates it with her abuse.

The fact is, your abuser tried to map your life for you. But he does not own you, and you have the freedom and the power to overcome and transcend the associations. You deserve to be happy, to be free of any feelings of shame or guilt or fear. You have the right to a completely satisfying sexual life. You are a righteous young woman. If you can get in touch with the feelings and consciously change the awful associations, you can re-map your life.

The feelings may not come all at once. That's perfectly normal. If you feel detached from your feelings as you begin to tell your story, so be it. Don't let anyone tell you that you have to connect with the feelings. You will do so when you are ready to do so. Sometimes connecting your heart and your mind would induce more pain than you could bear.

Eventually, feelings will begin to surface—usually some combination of fear, shame, and guilt. Let's look at these feelings squarely and see if we can begin to break their grip on you. And remember: Sexual abuse is *never* the fault of the survivor; it's always the fault of the abuser.

✳ ✳ ✳

Fear

"No one knows how far I've been pushed, and how I

hate the skeleton my flesh is walking around with. I carry

my fear like a rock in my heart."

—A TWENTY-YEAR-OLD SURVIVOR

Not surprisingly, fear is the most common response to sexual abuse—fear of what's happening, fear that someone will find out, fear of not knowing when your abuser will attack again, fear that the abuse will never end, fear that you'll be harmed if you tell, fear that you're damaged for life. You may even be afraid that abuse is your destiny. Incest, stranger rape, date rape, acquaintance rape, abuse by clergy/coach/mentor—any kind of sexual abuse carries the weight of fear along with it.

Abusers are usually really good at instilling fear. Maybe your cousin told you you're only worth being molested. Maybe your dad put such fear into you that you're afraid if you disclose the abuse, everyone in the family will suffer. Maybe he told you that your mother knows and has asked not to talk about it, or that your mother will blame you, or that it will break up the family.

Abusers set just such traps. The truth is, your abuser does not care if he hurts you. If he cared, he wouldn't abuse you. All he cares about is his fulfillment, his control, his needs. In the case of incest, you may feel love from him at times, and there may be moments when he is actually loving toward you, but his love is self-serving, and the trap he sets is often so tightly sealed that you feel there is no way out.

The first step toward overcoming the fear is to recognize that your abuser is responsible not only for the abuse, but also for the fear that accompanies it. He put it there, not you. Talking about your fear with a therapist or a friend can help you see that the fear was instilled in you and give you some distance from it.

When the abuse is over and your abuser is out of your life, keep reassuring yourself that he hurt you but that he is gone, and no one else will ever hurt you again in that way. You can try making a list of everything that gives you strength in the world. And remember that it's still all right to be afraid sometimes. Very often I find myself telling girls that it's fine to check under the bed before they go to sleep; it's fine to sleep with a stuffed animal or their pet; it's fine to check the locks on the door. If that's what you need to do to convince yourself that no one can get in, that no one can hurt you, do it. It's perfectly natural to feel fear. Talk about it, define it, and label it, and you will work through it.

Guilt

"God didn't love me. It didn't matter if I prayed before

I climbed into my little bed with the Power Rangers

sticker or not. I had already spent enough time thinking

it was my fault, that if I'd done something, just been

cleverer, I could have stopped him."

—A SEVENTEEN-YEAR-OLD INCEST SURVIVOR

Another emotion surrounding sexual abuse is guilt. If you are a survivor of incest, you might feel guilty for not having told anyone, and yet you cannot imagine having told. You might wonder why you didn't stop it. You might feel guilty about it. If you were date-raped while drunk or stoned, you might feel totally responsible for what happened.

In fact, the guilt can be pretty overwhelming, especially if you got any pleasure from the experience. Some girls' bodies can't help but respond to physical stimulation. That's just the way they're wired, and it's perfectly normal. But then they'll feel racked with guilt and wonder, "How could I have enjoyed this? What kind of horrible person am I?"

Other girls feel something, but it's not pleasure; it's sheer pain and terror. And still others will go numb, removing themselves from their bodies so they don't have to feel anything at all. I even know gynecologists who have reported seeing girls with bruised vaginas who had no memory of forced sex.

It's like having an ice cube put down your back. At first you feel the cold, but if more ice cubes are put down your back, you might become immune to the cold—after a while you might not feel it at all—but you still know the ice cubes are cold. Many incest survivors talk about being physically numb. Even some girls who have contracted herpes or STDs that cause physical discomfort say they are practically numb in the genital area.

Just remember: Whether you feel pleasure or pain or nothing at all, you didn't do this to yourself. It was done to you, usually in a thoroughly calculated way, and there is absolutely nothing to be guilty or ashamed of. Sexual abuse is never a girl's fault. Never. Even in cases of date rape, where you might actually have had some power to control the outcome, if you resisted or said no, the blame rests with your abuser, not with you.

Shame

"The shame covers me sometimes. I sit in the cold and refuse to close the window. I'll go out without a decent coat in the middle of winter. I'll sit somewhere shivering and not even consider just getting a sweater. I feel like I deserve this cold, this discomfort."

—A TWENTY-TWO-YEAR-OLD INCEST SURVIVOR

All survivors of incest at some point also feel shame. Other types of abuse cause girls to feel shame as well, but shame is embodied in the very nature of incest. Shame differs from guilt in subtle ways. Shame is not necessarily connected with the act itself; it's the secretiveness of it all that causes shame. After all, if it weren't something to be ashamed of, it wouldn't be such a big secret, right?

Shame usually brings on a kind of quiet numbing; it can seem to reach to the core of who you are, and you might even begin to believe that it defines you. You're sure that people can tell that your father or stepfather or brother is molesting you. You carry around that shame and eventually begin to believe that the shame exists because of you, because you're keeping this awful secret. You might try not to think about it, but it starts coming out in your dreams. You might walk around thinking that people would judge you, shun you, blame you if they knew.

The shame of incest is one of the most difficult emotions to overcome.

Time and again, it deters girls from telling. But believe me about this: Once you tell a trusted friend, relative, counselor, or therapist, the shame does begin to lift.

If you are the victim of incest, please understand that your father didn't start molesting you because of anything you said or did. He did it because he is a sick person with a totally warped idea of right and wrong. He tried to pull you into his demented reality. He undoubtedly planned how to get into a sexual situation with you. It was not your fault. You had no choice. This goes for other types of sexual abuse, too.

As you begin to face your abuse, you may feel despondent, depressed, and afraid of intimacy, but you don't need to feel bad or shameful. Your father/brother/uncle/acquaintance is the one who is sick and set a trap for you. When you begin to shed some of the shame, you begin to shed some of your sense of responsibility and vice versa, and that's vital for healing.

There is shame in all abuse. But the shame belongs to the act, not to you. It's very important to remember that someone committed an act of violence against you, and you could not stop it. It can be difficult to see this in relation to yourself. But think about other girls who are molested. Isn't it easy to see that it wasn't their fault? Wouldn't you tell them not to be ashamed? Do the same for yourself.

Other Aftershocks: Sex after Abuse

"My lover says, 'It's awfully crowded in here.' That's because

I carry my father with me."

—A TWENTY-YEAR-OLD INCEST SURVIVOR

Many sexually abused girls go on to have very complicated feelings about sex. Some girls report being promiscuous because this is their drive, to keep having meaningless sex because that's all they feel they are good for. They feel worthless, and so they go off with guy after guy and let themselves be used for sex and virtually feel nothing. But in fact, these girls are trying to gain power through these sexual liaisons. They are trying to overcome the feeling of powerlessness instilled by the sex abuse and "prove" that they can choose whom they have sex with.

Some girls get really freaked out if they have violent sexual fantasies. They can't believe they get turned on by fantasies of violence and feel a lot of shame about them. Or they fear that the only way they'll be able to get turned on is through being violently dominated. Just talking about this and admitting it, even on a hotline, can be really helpful. You are not alone. Many people who have been tortured have such fantasies. As long as you are open to looking at them and talking about them, they will pass. You will begin to understand that you are not a freak, and that you are simply responding to what's been done to you. Eventually, you will be relieved of the shame by getting more control over your fantasy life.

Many girls talk about being afraid to be touched, being afraid that if they are touched in the same way their abuser touched them, they might freak out. Some girls are afraid of physical intimacy. Others report feeling nothing when they are touched because they spent so long escaping their bodies during the abuse.

If any of this is happening to you, give yourself time. You can and will have healthy, loving, intimate, and sexual relationships after abuse.

Once you are in a relationship with a sensitive lover who understands (and if he/she doesn't, he/she's probably not the person for you!), refer them to a book by Laura Davis, *Allies in Healing: When the Person You Love Was Sexually Abused as a Child*. As the subtitle suggests, it has some wonderful insights for partners of girls and women who were sexually abused.

Let's get one thing clear right now: You are not damaged goods. You are entitled to a fine, satisfying sexual life—with someone who respects your boundaries. The act of sex, when accompanied by love and desire and deep attraction and connection, is the opposite of rape, sex abuse, and incest. So consider your first sexual love affair your first. Don't worry and don't be afraid if, in the beginning, you experience triggers and déjà vu. It's okay to take it slow and be honest with your partner, who respects you, about what you're feeling, and about how much touch and what kind of touch you are comfortable with. Those feelings will be replaced eventually with healthy sexual and sensual pleasures. Just give yourself time.

❈   ❈   ❈

Let Go

"I sealed myself off from my emotions, locked them in
a Ziploc bag, and put them in the freezer. Now I am ready to
defrost that frozen bag."

—A TWENTY-YEAR-OLD SURVIVOR OF DATE RAPE

However you choose to face and reveal your abuse—through your poetry or art or dancing or track, whether you've told one friend or many, told your parents or not—don't worry about how it's coming out. And don't worry if some days you want to talk about it a lot, and other days you don't want to talk about it at all. It's all okay. These are your feelings, and you get to determine what to do with them. You may feel embarrassed after telling people, or you may feel an incredible burden lifted right away. The bottom line is, by telling your story, you are letting go of the shame and the guilt that have been keeping you conflicted and full of self-doubt. You are building new road maps, undergoing a kind of metamorphosis, and taking back what the abuser tried to steal but never could. There is so much power in the simple act of speaking out.

Whatever your age, you are the right age to be coming out and telling your truth. Find someone to tell—and tell, tell, tell until your lungs ache. Tell until you can't tell anymore. It won't take away what happened to you, but it will re-map your life and take away the power from the abuse and the abuser. Read on—and remember, you are strong and resilient. And you are not alone.

PART TWO
BEFORE WE OPEN THE BOX

Chapter 5

Girls' Genius

How Girls Get through the Actual Abuse Experience

"While my father was molesting me, I would look at the wallpaper with all the little fairies. I would pretend they were my
friends, and that they were sprinkling fairy dust on me. I made up
names for all the fairies, and I was the queen fairy, and I could
protect every little girl in my world."

—A SEVENTEEN-YEAR-OLD INCEST SURVIVOR

If you are not a sexual-abuse survivor, you may be wondering how on earth
girls get through such experiences, but if you are a survivor, you probably
understand all too well. You too have lived through the unbearable and gotten up the next day and dragged yourself to school, sat through classes as if
nothing had happened, played on the soccer team, debated on the debate
team, created art or music or poetry. Somehow survivors learn how to live
with their abuse. They have to—it's the only way they can function.

One of my clients recounted an amazing dream she had several years
after the abuse had stopped, in which she was her younger self in her childhood bed. In the dream her father came to her as usual, got on top of her, and
started to have sex with her. As he started raping her, a part of her—what she
called her "transparent self"—got up out of the bed to watch "the girl" and
her father. Then she saw all these healing little angels surrounding the
girl on the bed. They lifted the father off her and made him disappear,
and then the hovering girl descended back onto the bed and melted into her
own body.

This dream depicts what many young women experience, whether consciously or unconsciously: leaving their bodies to survive their abuse. Clinically, this would be called "disassociation," and many inexperienced clinicians working with sex-abuse survivors think of this leaving the body, this floating, as a psychological problem. But as you'll learn in this chapter, not only is it not a problem, it is a lifeline, a brilliant strategy for trauma survival.

Some girls leave their bodies or create fantasy worlds; others focus all their mental energy on something in the room or outside the window as a way of walling themselves off from what's happening to their bodies. Girls have been known to count, catalog, sing silently, create a piece of art, choreograph a dance, memorize complex mathematical problems or lyrics, or project themselves into a painting on the wall—all ways of separating their minds from the situation.

In the coming pages, you will hear from Lily, who recounts envisioning herself as a heroine rescuing trapped children. Garnet will describe repeatedly singing the childhood song "Miss Mary Mac" in her head. Other girls will talk about focusing on the color of the wallpaper, the nuances of the light coming in through the window, the sounds of the birds outside. One of my clients even counted the flowers on her wallpaper until she reached the number 643. One girl talked about disappearing into a painting of a boat and sailing away. I spoke to one girl who had memorized the lyrics to an Italian opera. One of my clients even used a different name at work so she wouldn't have to identify with the soiled name her abuser-father called her.

Often the only way to get through traumas like these is not to feel. And that's exactly what these fantasy worlds allow: They give girls a place to go so they don't have to be present in their violated bodies.

In 1992 Judith Lewis Herman, one of the major contributors to the field of understanding sexual abuse, published a book called *Trauma and Recovery.* In this groundbreaking book, Herman compares the violence of being a war prisoner to the violence of being a sexual-abuse victim. She brilliantly brings out the similarities between being politically terrorized and sexually terrorized. She shows us that both types of survivors suffer through overwhelming feelings of guilt and shame, often with nowhere to go and no one to talk to about it. And so they turn inward. Soldiers in confinement have been known to survive by making obsessive lists or by counting. Girls do these same things while they are being abused. Their minds and spirits will invent fantastically creative ways to survive torture.

Herman discusses how the Vietnam War Memorial, by acknowledging the reality of all the war's death, suffering, and trauma, gave vets a kind of container for their pain. It gave their suffering credibility. My book is meant to be that memorial for sexual-abuse survivors—that proof of pain, that acknowledgment that you are still alive inside and out, even after your perpetrator tried to kill your spirit and rob you of your rights.

Creating Alterior Worlds

That doesn't mean it's easy to talk about your fantasy world. Girls know it can sound "a little crazy" to divulge the details of their fantasies. But in my work with girls, I have found that over time, as they become more comfortable talking about the abuse itself, they will usually reveal some strategy they used to get through it. If they ask me if I think they're crazy, I always reassure them that the worlds they created are a measure of their extraordinary resourcefulness, and that I admire their skill at surviving. The fact is, a girl's ability to go elsewhere during her sexual abuse, to create a safe, inviolable place for herself, only means that she won't allow her abuser to kill off her spirit. However much he may violate her, this is one thing he cannot steal.

Often a therapist will not fully understand these strategies. I have had several clients come to me after having worked with a therapist who wanted to help them "resolve" their fantasy "problem." But these girls knew intuitively that there was nothing at all wrong with their fantasizing, and that it was what had enabled them to get through the abuse. Their fantasies are like a baby's security blanket, accessible when they need them for comfort or to get through a transition, but not a substitute for reality.

Of course, some girls simply can't disappear into fantasies during molestation. If your father or molester keeps talking and talking or instructs you to do certain things, you have to stay present to be safe; you can't escape. For example, the uncle of one of my Asian clients used to make her go through a ritual of bowing down at his feet and reciting a statement that she worshipped and adored him and wanted to have his baby as soon as she came of age. During the molestation, he also forced her to repeat these things. Another client talked about her father's forcing her to comment on his body and male prowess continuously during the molestation. Often girls don't have the option of taking themselves away.

But girls who do have options use them. In this chapter, Zinnia and Lily will tell you about the amazing fantasy worlds they constructed to survive their rape and molestation. If you have any doubts about their sanity or your own, read on. These are remarkable, strong, courageous, and perfectly sane girls who used their minds to survive the unspeakable.

Zinnia

Zinnia is one of those girls whose experience was so brutal you may wonder how she survived it. It's hard to believe that a girl could be trapped with an abuser for ten years with no one to help her. Zinnia suffered this long-term incest at the hands of her stepfather. Her mentally ill mother knew about the abuse and didn't stop it. In her story, Zinnia takes us inside the elaborate fantasy world she created to escape from her stepfather time after time.

Zinnia came to me through the underground network of girls who bring their friends in for help. She had been working with kids at a camp when she broke down. She had seen a little boy try to put his hands down a little girl's pants and freaked out. She actually fainted. When she came to, she told her supervisor she felt ill and needed to go home. That night, she called a friend whom she knew had gotten some therapy and told her she was an incest survivor and was having flashbacks. She asked her friend to take her to her next therapy session.

I met Zinnia when she was twenty-three. A beautiful Mexican woman, she was tall and strong and articulate beyond her years. But when she began to talk about her abuse, her voice became very, very small. She said she was sorry to burden me with her story and explained that she'd thought it was all behind her. After all, the abuse had stopped four years earlier, and she had pressed charges already and had seen a court-appointed counselor for five sessions. She felt ashamed that she had more work to do.

I assured her that there was nothing to be ashamed of, and we began our treatment.

Zinnia told me that her mother is a schizophrenic, her stepfather an alcoholic, and she an only child. Zinnia's biological father abandoned the family soon after Zinnia's birth, and Zinnia was just six when her mother married a man who had already served a jail sentence for child molestation. He waited two years before starting to molest Zinnia. He continued to molest her until she was eighteen.

The family lived in an old trailer in a dirt-poor area of the Texas foothills. Her mother was on welfare, and her stepfather never worked. Zinnia often went without food. When she entered school and spoke only Spanish, she was put into special education.

But she proved the school wrong and went on to become a perfect student. That was Zinnia's MO. During those many years when she was being molested, Zinnia showed only a perfect girl to the world: a perfect student, a perfect friend, a perfect daughter. She did exactly as she was told, and she took care of her sick mother as well as she could.

Until she went to college, that is. During her freshman year, she tried to kill herself with an overdose of pills. Luckily, her roommate found her in time, and in the hospital, Zinnia told social services about her home life. Her stepfather was arrested and arraigned, and her mother was put into psychiatric treatment.

Zinnia has been in therapy with me for the past four years, and it has been a real roller-coaster ride. Because she finds it so difficult to trust anyone, it was a full year before Zinnia opened up to me and had any faith that the therapy could help her.

When she started therapy, she had never been in a relationship, and she was terrified to let anyone get to know her, including me. Now, at twenty-seven, she is in a doctoral program in social work on a full scholarship at Columbia University. She has slowly begun to date and has developed new friendships. She is passionate about her work and wants to help socially disadvantaged children. I believe Zinnia will reach and save many children. I also believe that her story and depth of honesty will help incest survivors come out the other side, knowing they are not alone.

{ *Zinnia's Story* }

Building Houses, Building Dreams

All through my childhood, I was the one in charge of things. At least, that was the illusion I liked to maintain. I had control. Of course, I knew this control was only available to me as long as I didn't shake things up, as long as I played my role. This role included being quiet about the rapes I suffered for ten long years at the hands of my drunk, old, disgusting stepfather. The first time he attacked me, he must have been at least seventy already. I was alone in the trailer with him. I was around eight. He approached me, pinned me down on the dirty couch, and put his fingers inside my vagina, forcing his dirty, drunk mouth on mine. When he was done with me, he pushed me aside.

When my mother came home that night, she found me huddled in a corner shaking and crying. I told her what had happened. I pleaded with her to help me, but she just stared back at me blankly and said, "Look, he helps us with money. Just try not to put up so much of a fight." I knew my mother was crazy, but I had no idea she'd make me put up with this. She heard voices that weren't talking and saw people who weren't there, but she was all I had. So I began my retreat.

I ignored the smell of cat pee everywhere, the dirty dishes always filling the sink, the overgrown lawn, and the empty cupboards, but I couldn't ignore my stepfather. I remember the gun closet, repository of the switch and the rifles. These were the weapons my stepfather threatened to hurt me with if I told the authorities about him. Tell the authorities? That was the last thing I wanted. I just wanted to be as walled off as possible from everyone. I couldn't imagine that anyone would ever take care of me.

I retreated deeply into books and school. I would stay after school whenever possible and read until the building closed at 6:00 PM I joined the Girl Scouts, then the 4-H Club. As I got older,

I was on the swim team, the debate team, the cheerleading squad, school government—anything to keep me away from home.

I tried everything I could think of to stay away from my stepfather, but he managed to corner me and mess with me whenever he could get his hands on me. But when I hit adolescence, I began to fight back. I started keeping a knife under my pillow so that if he came to me in the middle of the night in a drunken stupor, I could pull it on him and threaten him. Sometimes that worked, and he'd leave me alone. But it wasn't always that easy. A lot of times he would just sneak up behind me and pull me to him in situations where I could not get away. Even though he was an old man by then, he was still very strong because he had been a construction worker.

Trying to get help from my mother was completely hopeless. By this time, she was hearing voices almost all the time and could barely bathe herself. I knew that my mother had no right to demand my complicity—she was the adult, the parent—and yet it was crystal clear that she was incapable of protecting me.

My mother told me that I could handle the molestations because I was an "old soul." She said I was a soul who had lived many lives in many places, endured many things, and would continue on. I almost felt as if people would be able to see it when they looked at me, all that pain, all that time, all those centuries of living and dying locked behind my child's eyes.

But no one seemed to notice.

And all the while I was sleeping at night with a knife under my pillow, scared to death that that disgusting old man would rape me again. I kept winning academic and sports awards at school. Talk about a split reality.

Starting when I was really young, I had these secret little worlds that I would escape to. I would imagine myself as different people with complex personalities. I saw myself as strong, protected, and able.

Even when I was little and curled up under the covers and would hear him come in and smell the cigarettes and beer on his breath and his dirty, smelly clothes, and know what was coming next, I would retreat to my little world of cleanness and perfection and keep myself safe.

I would pretend to be asleep—he didn't care—and would invent a new fantasy world each time. By the time he finished with me, I could fall asleep peacefully because I was no longer a scared little girl in a run-down trailer; I was a princess on an island, a warrior queen, a waif turned into a strong beauty. I was in control.

I would transport myself to beautiful places. I had a friend who lived in a beautiful house, and when I'd go over there, I would pore over the magazines and catalogs I found lying around in the living room. That's why my fantasy houses were always so beautiful. They would have sparkling clean floors and windows, beautiful curtains swaying in the breeze, fresh flowers, and clean rugs.

Sometimes I would imagine myself in a garden full of lilacs, honeysuckle, mimosas, peonies, orchids, roses, and magnolias. I'd never actually seen magnolias, but I loved the word and would roll it around in my mind. I imagined how magnolias looked and smelled. What I thought about didn't matter, as long as it kept my brain engaged.

I would also transport myself to the places I read about in books, changing them if I didn't like certain parts, adding extra bits to keep my mind engaged. I loved reading about horses, and I liked to imagine myself on an island with no one else around, no cars or streets or stores or schools, just a big house full of white things, and open windows and horses outside on the grass. Or I would be in a cozy cabin in the woods, having to fend for myself. Of course, I had built the cabin myself. I'd have Herculean powers, and I would be able to chop down trees, too. I'd pick wild strawberries and catch fish in a stream for food. I made up fairylands and mythical landscapes.

When my brain ran out of fantasy material or just refused to go that far away, I would picture words in my head: L-I-L-A-C B-U-S-H-E-S. Then I'd count the letters and spaces in the words and picture them being slammed out by a typewriter's keys. Any time I had an empty moment that could be filled with something painful, I would take words, phrases from television ads, and entire sentences, and count, count, count, count.

After I would hear his footsteps leave my room, I would keep counting until I fell asleep. Even now, at twenty-seven, I can retreat to some better, safer place in my mind if I need to. And sometimes my fantasy has me going back to that scared little girl huddled in the night and putting my arms around her and holding her and telling her she'll be all right.

My fantasy worlds saved me; there is no doubt in my mind. I was the angel keeping myself alive.

My Thoughts

Zinnia kept herself alive spiritually and physically by using her brain and her imagination. When she moved out and went off to college, everything fell apart—and everything came together. She suddenly gained clarity about the abuse. It took moving away and being on her own for that to happen. That's when she could afford to feel. And once she was no longer on autopilot, once she didn't have to keep it all together just to make it through the day, she realized how truly horrendous her experience had been. And that is when and why she attempted suicide.

This scenario is common: Girls have some sort of breakdown or shatter emotionally after they leave the abusive home. While they're still living under the same roof with their abuser, they simply can't afford to fully feel or to process what's happening. But after they leave and can let down their guard, they fall apart.

This is also often the time when girls come to see me, once they are out of imminent danger and can begin to process their abuse.

Lily

When I met Lily, she was eighteen, living on her own, and working full-time. She said she was in love with her partner, a young woman of twenty. They had a good sexual connection that was not at all threatening to Lily, but she was not able to be intimate with her partner emotionally and wanted to get to the bottom of her problems with intimacy. She was in a loving, supportive relationship, but she was terrified. Lily survived abuse from the ages of seven through fifteen at the hands of her biological uncle and cousin.

Lily talked about being certain that she was gay but still going out to bars and cruising guys. She wanted closeness in her relationship, but she kept pulling away. Lily had never shared with anyone that she was molested throughout her childhood and young adolescence. She guarded her secret fiercely, until one day she broke down and confided in a good friend. This good friend happened to be one of my clients, so she brought Lily in to see me.

During her years of abuse, Lily often inhabited an elaborate fantasy world with very specific details. She could spend hours upon hours in this world. In Lily's world, she was the most wonderful, interesting, diversified superhero you could ever imagine. In the "real" world, of course, she was a frightened little girl with no power. When I met Lily, she knew that her fantasy world had saved her, but she also knew it was time to join the "real" world.

I have worked with Lily for two years now. She still retreats to her fantasy world when she needs to, and she has done some amazing healing. She is a member in good standing in our world, and our world is better for having young women like Lily in it.

{ *Lily's Story* }

A Superhero Beyond Superheroes

Ever since I can remember, I have loved my imagination. As a child, I loved to spend hours alone in my room, where I could escape into my own little world of dolls and books and colors and safety. I would make little dollhouses out of shoeboxes and streets out of colored paper.

I remember the first time I was molested. I was about seven years old and was alone in my room, working on one of my creations. My teenage cousin came in to say goodnight before he went home for the evening. He came over to me and kissed me, and then he put his hand down my shirt and squeezed and grinned at me. It felt weird, but I liked this cousin, and I just let it go.

My mom was working two jobs. My parents had divorced when I was two, and I don't really remember my father. He left the country and went back to Trinidad, where we were all from. There were always relatives in and out of our house, and lots of different people were left in charge of my care. This particular male cousin used to have me sit on his lap while we watched TV. At some point, he started putting his hands down my shirt and pants. I would try to wiggle away, but he would tell me that this is what cousins did. He told me it was my fault he was doing it, and that my mother would only get mad if I told her.

I'm not sure why I didn't tell my mom, probably because I didn't see her all that much. She was usually sleeping when I left for school and gone when I returned home. My mother was also a really devout Christian and always said that sex was dirty and I'd better stay away from it. So whenever relatives were looking after me, I would just try to spend as much time as possible alone in my room.

When I was around twelve, my cousin's dad, my uncle, forced oral sex on me. My uncle and cousin went right on abusing me until I was fifteen and had the physical strength and the guts to get them to stop. Until then, their threats that I would be sent back to Trinidad were enough to keep me silent. But I felt like a used rag doll.

That's why I created a world where I was strong and brave and could fight off anyone. I made up different names for myself. Sometimes I was Truth, sometimes I was Victory, but I always killed the bad guys.

In this world of mine, I did all sorts of things that a real person couldn't possibly do. In my fantasy world, people liked and respected me for my character, not my looks. I was skinny, not too tall, attractive but not beautiful. I was attractive in a way that people wouldn't necessarily notice at first, but I would become more beautiful as they got to know me.

In "real life," I was serious, well behaved, and quiet—but a strong kind of quiet. The fantasy me could be really funny, the kind of funny that everyone loves to be around. I had a very sharp tongue. I was also very mysterious. I loved that there were many things about me that people didn't know. For example, in my fantasies I was this amazing singer. I could sing opera, blues, and jazz. I could sing like Bessie Smith and Billie Holiday and Aretha Franklin. I knew everything there was to know about music. People would come to me from all over the world with questions about music, and I would gladly give them the answers.

I could also fight very well. I was an expert boxer, and I had the highest belt in the martial arts. I knew how to use a gun and had incredible aim. I think I got this from cowboy movies such as *Rio Bravo*, which I loved. I had a great love for animals, and I could communicate with them. I could speak dog language, kitty language, bird language, and monkey language. I knew what these animals needed from me. And naturally, that was almost always to save them from some cruel human who wanted to hurt them in some way. Of course, I always succeeded.

In my world, I could predict the weather. I knew what people were thinking before they did. I was all powerful. I was able to take care of myself and anyone else who needed my help.

I also created this school in my mind, and that's where most of the fantasies took place. I worked in the school and ran it behind the scenes. There were other teachers and students, all of whom had names and personalities. There were classrooms and assemblies in the auditorium and everything. Whenever a child needed help, if they were hurt or hungry, they were sent to me. I helped them; I brought them back to health; I entertained them and made them happy.

As I got older, the stories I made up became more elaborate; my powers grew. Sometimes I would be called away from the school because I would be needed somewhere in the world. If there were cornfields on fire in Mexico, I would be called there. I would fly off and put out the fires. I would put up tents for the people who were displaced and arrange for airplanes to drop food and water. I would rebuild their fire-ravaged towns and cities. And then I would go on to my next adventure. People were always thanking me and telling me how much they loved me and appreciated me. That really made me feel good inside.

I would get ideas from places I had seen on TV or that I had been to. For instance, the school had a large wooden spiral staircase with ornate carvings of cherubs, just like the one I had seen at a mansion we once visited on a field trip. The wood was maple and smelled like the outdoors. The floors were shiny marble with hairline designs of deep black. I could imagine the sound of the children's footsteps on the marble. There were paintings on the ceiling. The paintings were like Michelangelo's and were of beautiful, muscular bodies.

Sometimes I would memorize the bone structure of one of the figures in the paintings on the ceiling. Sometimes I would imagine how some of the people in my world walked or ran. I would imagine them running in slow motion. I would see the hair on their heads move with the breeze. I would picture the minute details of their expressions.

I lived in this fantasy world much of the time, though I could always bring myself back to "reality" if I had to. When I graduated from high school and moved out and began to support myself,

I was able to be in the "real" world more and more. But even now, when I have bad memories of my cousin or uncle, I find myself becoming Victory, swooping down and catching a falling baby in midair, and bringing her to safety.

My Thoughts

Like many girls, Lily and Zinnia both figured out ways to stay whole while their molesters were raping them. They know that their fantasy worlds saved them. They see the characters as their saviors. They know that they saved themselves, perhaps not in body, but in spirit.

Because Lily could not save herself from her cousin or her uncle, she saved hundreds of children and villages. Because she could not have a voice during her rapes, she imagined herself singing as well as any blues singer. Because she could not get away, she could fly and scoop up falling children. I learned through Lily that all girls are superheroes during and after their molestations. You are the superhero—saving yourself. And you deserve credit for getting through however you can.

Because Zinnia lived in a dirty, run-down trailer, she was able to build a home in the woods that was clean and fresh and beautiful. You see, that's what girls do. They find places to go to, worlds to discover, plants to count, lyrics to memorize, mathematical problems to solve, people to save, because they are resourceful and resilient and courageous.

Don't let anyone ever tell you that you were crazy for leaving your body. Just know that you were taking care of yourself. Don't let anyone tell you this is denial. It is survival. When we're so unsafe, we have to create our own safety. Lily told me that sometimes at night, she can't sleep and the memories come back. When that happens, she just puts on her superhero cloak and saves a hurting child, and soon she is asleep and dreaming sweetly.

PART THREE

OPENING PANDORA'S BOX:
GIRLS TELL THEIR STORIES

Chapter 6

The Deepest Wound

Father-Daughter Incest

"The little girl in me died the moment he forced himself inside."

—AN EIGHTEEN-YEAR-OLD SURVIVOR OF INCEST

As Coral spoke, her eyes were dead, her voice was monotonous, and it was as if she were telling me of some far-off experience that she had watched from the sidelines, rather than the experience of being sexually molested by her father from the time she was twelve until she turned eighteen. Twenty-two years old, Coral sat in my office and told me about the time she was fifteen and her father took her into his art studio before dinner, opened his pants, and pushed her head to him. After he climaxed and wiped himself off, Coral washed her face, and they went around the block to their home and sat down to dinner with Coral's mother. What was so chilling was not just that her father was abusing her, but also that the abuse was so thoroughly integrated into Coral's family life.

Coral is one of the many courageous young women who have come to my private practice through an underground network of sexual-abuse survivors. What Coral experienced—for a period of six years—was incest.

What Is Incest?

What, exactly, is incest? Incest is forced sexual contact with a family member. As with all sexual abuse, incest is a sexualized relationship between two people in which one has the power to coerce and the other does not. Some incestuous behavior involves touch, some does not; it can be a one-time experience or go on for many years. Being forced to engage in unwanted genital touching or fondling, being made to look at a relative's private parts or to show yours, being asked to pose nude for photos, or being penetrated—all of these acts violate the boundary between adult and child, or child and child.

Father, stepfather, brother, stepbrother, uncle, cousin, foster father, even a mother—all can be perpetrators of incest. Even a sexual experience with a close family friend can have some of the same effects as incest. Whenever someone you trust as "family" violates you in this way, it's incest.

One sixteen-year-old incest survivor described her experience like this: "I see him walk toward me and try to think of an escape, but there is no safe place, and now it is too late. As he reaches out for me, I simply fall to the floor, which is no longer strong enough to hold me up."

If you are an incest survivor, maybe you've had that feeling that you were about to fall through the floor, and that your world couldn't hold you up, either. That's what happens when someone you trust or depend on violates you sexually.

While incest is usually not as violent as other sexual violations, like stranger rape or date rape, of all forms of abuse, it usually creates the deepest wound. Of course, it *can* involve force, but often it is something that happens over time and involves a lot of seduction, manipulation, bribery, and lies. Fathers, especially, will often take their time convincing their daughters that the incest is their destiny. They will manipulate their daughters into believing that they don't have a choice. This "destiny" line is just one of many myths that surround incest. Let's take a look at some of the others.

Myths and Truths about Incest

MYTH: "I need you to have sex with me because your mother won't." One popular myth is that men demand sex from their daughters because they are not "getting any" from their wives. Some men even go so far as to say, "Your mother would want you to do this because she wants me to be fulfilled, and she's too ill/busy to meet my sexual needs."

TRUTH: In fact, the clinical information we have is that men who molest their daughters usually continue to have sex with their wives.[1] It goes without saying, of course, that regardless of whether they are "getting any" from their wives, they have no right to abuse their daughters.

MYTH: "It's my job to teach you how to be a good lover." Some girls are told that it's their father's job to teach them how to be a good lover.

TRUTH: Not only is it not the father's job to teach his daughter to be a good lover, but in a healthy father-daughter relationship, a father will be very hesitant and a bit uncomfortable to go into any discussion of his adolescent daughter's sexual relationships. There are usually appropriate boundaries around these issues.

MYTH: Girls seduce their fathers *or* "You're so tempting (in those shorts, that dress), I *have* to have sex with you!"

TRUTH: Not only do girls not seduce their fathers, but they need their fathers to see them as their "little girls." This helps a girl develop trust in family boundaries and thus in the world. When her father does not sexualize her, she feels more secure and less objectified. The last thing a girl desires is to seduce her father. This is a frightening distortion.

MYTH: Young girls are very attracted to older men—their fathers, uncles, teachers, you name it. This myth is constantly being fed by Hollywood. Many films continue to show teen girls falling in love with men in their forties and older. Helped by the publication of Vladimir Nabokov's *Lolita* in 1955 (which, by the way, has been made into a movie not just once, but twice), in which a pubescent girl seduces her pathetically unlovable mother's boarder (substitute father figure) with her naive sexuality, we have held onto the myth that girls are often desperately attracted to older men.

TRUTH: There's a big difference between things like acknowledging your budding curves and feeling the first blush of sexual feelings and preying on older men. And men should be mature enough to realize it. The myth that a child wants sex with her father or a father figure is, simply put, a lie perpetuated through film and literature and a general cultural sexualization of children. But because girls really want to trust and believe the adults in their lives, it's easy for men to take advantage of their vulnerability.

The book *Reading Lolita in Tehran* by Azar Nafisi compares how the character Lolita was forcibly sexualized to how Iranian women are completely subjugated to men. Clearly, incest is a form of patriarchal control.

Coral

Coral came to see me when she was in her early twenties. She was ten years old when her father started being sexually inappropriate with her, eleven when he started molesting her, and eighteen when the molesting stopped because she got out of the house.

From the beginning, her father told her that she needed him, and that it was obvious from the way she dressed and looked that she really *wanted* him to sexually arouse her. When Coral started developing, he actually said that having her under the same roof was "like putting spaghetti in front of a hungry man. Of course he'll want to eat it!"

About three years ago, Coral and her boyfriend got my name through a friend of a friend in my underground network of incest survivors. When they called me, Coral had just revealed the incest to her mother, who was now coming from Europe to see her.

Coral's boyfriend accompanied her to her first session. She was tormented by her past and afraid that she would never get over her incest. She explained that her boyfriend was the first person she'd ever told. The second was her mother, and the third was me.

In that first session, I learned that Coral was twenty-two and had just graduated with honors from UC Berkeley with a degree in literature. She told me that she had just completed a book of poetry. She was having trouble enjoying anything these days, though, she said, because she felt tormented about her father. Her father now had AIDS, and she was terrified that she had it, too, even though she had taken an AIDS test and it was negative.

As she sat in my office picking at her fingernails and looking down at the floor, Coral rattled off her anxieties: "I'm having nightmares and these awful headaches. I pick my nails and skin and grind my teeth when I sleep. I wake up in cold sweats, I'm afraid to deal with my mother, who is coming next week. She is totally dependent and a mess. I can't stand anyone touching me. I'm jumpy about everything. I cry at the drop of a hat."

※　※　※

Even before she confessed to feeling like a basket case, I explained to her that whatever had happened was not her fault. I had to repeat it at least five times. At first Coral sat frozen; then she finally broke down and sobbed.

Now, three years after Coral first heard those words—"It's not your fault"—she wants every girl who has survived incest to know "it's not your fault, either."

{ *Coral's Story* }

Cats in the Courtyard

My father took away my adolescence. It started in Greece when I was ten, but the first time he raped me was after we moved to Holland, when I was twelve. From the ages of eleven to eighteen, I was abused by my father sexually on a regular basis. I was forced to perform oral sex, to receive it, and to have intercourse with him whenever he demanded it.

My father is a professor. He is egocentric and has a major persecution complex, but he has cultivated a public image of being very intelligent and wise and calm. He always had some strange theory, but he was an intellectual, and so people just accepted that he was a bit weird. There was this aura around him, like he was a Zen monk or something.

At home he could not keep up the persona. At home he was less guarded and felt entitled to be moody, controlling, and belligerent. He basically ruled our house. His thoughts were the right thoughts, and my mother and I had to attend to his every mood and desire. He was very forceful in expressing his opinions—so much so that you felt that if you did not agree with him, something in you was inferior. He told us which classical music was superior and things like that, and there was simply no discussion. What he said ruled.

My mother was a seamstress who catered to his every whim. She took care of the house, cooked our meals, woke me up in the morning, and put me to bed. I remember getting a lot of love from her, and I remember her love as fun love. Unlike my father, she was never smothering, telling me what I could and could not do, and she played with me a lot.

I have a lot of blank spots in my memories of my childhood. From what I have pieced together with the help of therapy, I know that when I was a child, my father never played with me, though he could be playful. He'd joke with me at times, and he always encouraged me to draw. But the truth is, I was on my own a lot as a child. I can remember one summer when I was about six years old, my parents tied the house key to a string and put it around my neck. I was to entertain myself during the day and return home by evening.

It has taken me years of therapy to realize that my mother was very afraid of life. What she thought she'd found in my father was a support system; with him she did not have to think on her own. It's pretty clear to me that my father mattered more to my mother than I did. She would rush around to get dinner on the table for him every night, even though he said she didn't have to cook if she didn't want to. She knew that if dinner was not on the table when he expected it, he would go on and on about how hungry he was and how he was a better cook anyway and all that. I learned early on that what he said was not always what he meant. He may have said we did not have to do certain things, but there was never really any choice.

I watched this very closely and learned that the rule of our house was to not upset Daddy. He had an explosive temper, and at times he would throw fits, screaming and breaking things. My father was a master at manipulating reality. As long as we did what he wanted us to do, the household would run smoothly.

When I was very young, my father would leave for months at a time to attend university lectures in other countries, and my mother and I would bond. I would sleep in the big bed with her, which was a huge treat. When I climbed into her bed, I felt very safe and cozy. We would play and eat when we wanted to, travel where and when we wanted to, and just relax.

These were also the years when my parents let me spend summers at my paternal grandmother's. I remember those summers as fun and playful. My grandmother lived in the countryside, and I played with my young cousins and all the animals. As I got older, I stopped spending summers there. I don't know why.

At some point, my mother started being the one who traveled at times. She would leave for a week at a time, visiting family in South Africa. I don't actually remember sleeping in the big bed with my father (this is one of my memory gaps), but I think it was assumed that when Mother traveled I would sleep with Daddy, just as I did with her when he was away.

When I was ten years old, my father starting holding me just a little too long when he would hug me. I don't have any clear memory of being sexualized at ten, but things definitely got uncomfortable. I know he used to have me sit on his lap a lot. The first time he abused me sexually I was eleven; at least, that's the first time I remember clearly. We were still living in Greece. I remember staring out the window at the garden downstairs, when he came up behind me and touched my breasts under my shirt. I was wearing white summer pants and a little red top that I really loved. It had little bows on the side. I was wearing little white shoes with black dots. I even remember the underwear I was wearing. I was just starting to develop breasts, and I felt really good in my pretty outfit.

I loved all animals, and I loved watching the cats in the courtyard as they played. As I stared at the cats, my father french-kissed me. My legs started shaking. I was supposed to go to a piano lesson, but he took me to his bed and performed oral sex on me. I remember shaking all over and just focusing on the thought, "Soon I will be at my piano lesson." I don't remember exactly what he said to me, but I know he was telling me that what he was doing would feel really good. I don't think I said anything.

I was shaking the whole way to the piano lesson, and when I got there, I couldn't play the music, I was shaking so much. I don't think he did anything else for a while after that, though he may have tried to initiate something at other times that year, because I do remember his complaining that I was always going off with my mother and did not give him much chance to be alone with me.

He raped me for the first time when I was twelve. We were living in Holland by then. My memories of it are like a sped-up film. He started to kiss me and I fought with him, and I told him I did not like this, and that I was a virgin and wanted to remain one. But he kept insisting that this was what I needed to do. He got angry. He screamed, "Enough of this!" and then stood up and pushed me and said, "Get naked and get in bed, now." I went into the bathroom and stayed there; then I got into my pajamas and got into my bed. He came and got me and put me in his bed, then climbed in, too. I was wearing my underwear and socks and three t-shirts under my pajamas; he was naked. I kept turning away from him and rolling onto my side.

I don't remember how one thing led to another, but at some point he took off my clothes, put a condom on, and began raping me. I was screaming and he covered my mouth. At that point, I was present (I hadn't taught myself to leave my body yet), and I was in excruciating pain. Afterward, he teased me and laughed at me and asked me why I was making such a fuss.

We hadn't been in Holland long, and I was having a hard enough time as it was. I did not speak English or Dutch. I had no family there, no friends; I really stood out with my dark skin and kinky hair. I had no protection or resources. My father could be so persuasive. He said that having sex with me was the natural way of things, and he cited all these examples of animals in the animal kingdom who are initiated into sex by their fathers. He babbled on about rituals and coming of age. He said that in the Jewish religion there is a ceremony called a Bat Mitzvah to celebrate the transition from child to woman, and that he wanted to initiate me into womanhood by having sex with me.

Thus began my father's invasion of my body and my soul. Any chance he got, he had intercourse with me, and/or forced oral sex. Because my life at home was a living hell, I built an elaborate other world, a fantasy world, and I had easy access to it. This world had elaborate characters with complicated story lines, in most of which I was a heroine saving abused orphans. In this other world, I was always strong and invincible. Although I am not aware that I was able to enter the fantasy world while I was being abused, I do know I got deep comfort from knowing that I could be back in that world at any moment. It seems I was always in that world when I was at home.

When I asked him why he was doing this to me, he said, "That's like putting a plate of spaghetti in front of a hungry man and asking him why he wants to eat it."

It took me a long time to realize how much that line affected me. It must have been my fault; after all, I was the spaghetti. It must have been my fault I had started to develop and was getting more attention from males.

He also said one thing that really got to me: He said that mothers know; they just do not discuss it with their daughters. He convinced me that my mother knew and was fine with it. When my mother would leave for her trips and say, "Take care of Daddy," I began to assume that this was some kind of secret code and she really did know what was happening. Everything felt really crazy and unsafe.

I found some friends—the kids you might call rejects—and I embraced punk culture. I related to the angry ideas groups like the Sex Pistols were expressing through their music. I was always fighting with teachers, always getting into trouble. But then I'd go home and have to deal with my father's sexual demands, and there I'd be, this passive little girl, just waiting for it to end.

The one time I refused to comply, my mother was away on a five-day trip. I think I was fourteen at the time. I screamed, "No! I will not! Keep away from me!" and ran to my room and locked the door. There was a way to lock my door with a key from the outside, and my father actually locked me in my room and told me I had to stay in there without food or water until I came to my senses. I stayed in my room for at least a day and a half, until I felt faint and had to eat or drink something. Then I gave in and asked him to let me out.

Before I could even eat or shower, he raped me. After that experience of being locked in my room, I figured it would be easier to just let it happen, and then it would be over with and I could get on with things. I learned to leave my body and go somewhere else during the rapes. I'd go numb. My body would not respond or get pleasure.

I kept hoping each time would be the last time for a while. From what I can piece together, I was doing a pretty good job of protecting my psyche from what was going on; I was kind of splitting off the incest from my feeling life. I went out with my mother whenever I could and I tried never to be alone with my father.

Sometimes my father would talk to me during the rapes. Sometimes his voice was like a buzz in the background; other times I remember him saying that he was a really good lover, and how lucky I was to have him as a lover. But I was always numb. Sometimes he would not say anything, and sometimes he would tell me that I didn't have to do it if I didn't want to. But the one time I asked not to, he became cold and angry, and when my mother came home, he made up some lies about bad behavior on my part and gave us all a really hard time. It was clear to me that I was better off just doing what he demanded. The few times he did not force me, he took it out on my mother and on me, becoming even more controlling.

When I was sixteen, he encouraged me to have a boyfriend, and I actually did. His name was James. We were not sexual, except for kissing. My father encouraged me to talk about James. I gave him minimal information, but he always pushed. One evening, after raping me, my father said, "Go out with James. Have fun." Unbeknownst to me, my father had given me this huge hickey, and when I met up with James, of course he noticed it right away. He asked where I got it, but I wouldn't say, so he broke up with me. My father always had ways of trapping me like that.

What makes me so angry now is that I realize how much he knew and how much I did not know, and how much I was giving him while he had absolutely no regard for me as a human being. That is the ultimate affront to the human spirit.

I used to think that my mother was not to blame. After all, I never told her about the abuse. But a memory that came back to me during therapy changed my view of her.

When I was about fourteen, my father needed a photo of himself for a magazine cover and decided to have me stand naked in front of him. He would be dressed all in black, his eyes closed. He had my mother take the picture. You could not make out my face, but my body was clearly visible. The idea was that the artist can resist the temptation of the naked woman. Through my therapy, I realized that my mother was really a co-conspirator.

My therapy has helped me to realize that I had no options during my childhood and adolescence, and that the incest was not my fault. I now understand that my mother was weak and would not protect me. Also, there was no modesty allowed in my home. My parents walked around naked and expected me to do so as well. I was ridiculed by both of them if I expressed a desire to behave modestly. I did anyway. There was not even a door on the bathroom. When I was twelve years old and wanted a bathing suit top, my mother teased me and said that I was to continue to go topless at the beaches.

Coming to California for college when I was eighteen, I felt like an immigrant from the beginning of the twentieth century, when everyone came here from war-torn or poverty-stricken places. I was out of my own private war zone at last. The first couple of years were especially difficult for me. I spent a lot of time numb or floating and would spout my father's belief systems about literature, music, and politics. His influence was huge and inescapable.

Even though I've been free of my parents for several years now, I still hear my father's voice inside my head controlling me at times. As the years move on, his voice is quieter and quieter. My therapist assures me that someday it will be so faint I will barely hear it.

Getting some perspective has helped me to begin to forgive myself. I still feel depressed at times. During my adolescence, I developed severe headaches and frequent nausea, which I continue to suffer from. Some days I feel worthless. But I realize now that as a child and adolescent, I did my best to keep myself alive. My mother was passive and frightened of the world. My father defined her every move. He molded her and tried to mold me, too. But with me he did not succeed.

It's taken a while, but I have begun to see things through my own eyes. I have started to hear my own voice. Three years ago, I changed my name so I would no longer have to share a name with my father. I will never go back to Holland, and I will never go back to what my life was. I have choices and freedoms, and I accept my incest as something that has happened to me. But it no longer defines who I am.

At the time I was being molested, I thought I was the only one. My father controlled everything in our house, and he always said that what was happening to me was natural, and that I should accommodate him. Even though I have to look back sometimes, I am moving forward. And even though it's painful for me to face my mother's complacency, doing so has helped me understand that it wasn't my fault. If I could have read something at the time about sex abuse, if people had talked openly about it, I could have been saved many years of guilt and shame and secrecy. Each time I talk about my incest, I get rid of some of that shame and guilt. Each person I share with, no matter what their response, takes another piece of the pain away. If my story has reached you, I am forever grateful.

My Thoughts

Even after Coral moved out of her house, her father still had power over her. For three years after her move to California, she still did work for him, keeping up with lectures he was interested in, meeting with American professors, networking for him .

It wasn't until he sent her a pornographic version of "Little Red Riding Hood" that she snapped. She called him to say she would not translate the story and said, "I think you know why!" Then she started sobbing and cried over and over again into the phone, "Why did you hurt me? Why did you hurt me?" Of course he did not answer. They hung up.

A few minutes later, Coral's mother called her, demanding to know why Coral would not help her father. It was then that she told her mother about the incest, and she urged her mother to get out of the house. Her mother was ready to leave, and she did. That was three years ago, and Coral has not spoken to her father since. She never confronted him about the incest directly.

Through therapy, Coral began to understand how both she and her mother were controlled by her father.

She began to see her mother's silent complicity regarding the incest and now understands her true place and function in the family. She was the sacrificial lamb, her father's sexual object. And she served an important function for her mother, serving her father's every need when her mother wasn't there to do so. (It's important to note that throughout the years of incest, her father never stopped having sex with his wife or with prostitutes, from whom he contracted AIDS.)

After Coral disclosed her sexual abuse to her mother, her mother admitted that the marriage had disintegrated, and that her father was having sex with young prostitutes on a regular basis. Then her mother told her that her father had AIDS. She even admitted that she had continued having sex with her husband *knowing* he had AIDS.

Coral's mother had grown up in a household without a father and with an emotionally abusive mother. Coral's mother never had insight into her own home situation or sought any sort of counseling. At twenty, she married the first man who asked her, simply to get out of her mother's house.

When Coral asked her mother what she would have done if she had told her about the incest as a child, she replied, "I really don't know. I can't say for sure that I would have left him."

Coral's mother claims to love her, and I believe that she does—as much as she can love anyone. But this love has many limitations. She was never really capable of parenting Coral. Coral was left on her own from a very young age, and her mother was completely complicit in the incest. She did nothing to protect her daughter. She left Coral alone with her father for weeks at a time, even when Coral begged her not to travel without her. Never once did she tell Coral that she had choices.

Coral has described many incidents when her mother failed to prevent her father from exercising his many forms of control and abuse. There was the time Coral describes in her own words, when she was around twelve and was trying on bathing suits. Her mother called her father in to see the suits, and he just laughed and said, "She will be topless on the beach!" So her mother took the tops away from Coral.

Holidays were never celebrated in Coral's home. Once, when friends brought over a birthday cake for Coral, her father ridiculed her and her mother for participating in such a ridiculous ritual. Coral's mother told her she could not have a birthday cake again.

And then there was Coral's high school graduation. She wanted very much to attend, but her father forbade it, and her mother backed him up. Coral could not receive her degree unless she attended, so in the end she did; of course, she was one of the only graduates there without a family member in attendance.

Through Coral's story, we come to understand how a girl who is strong and directed can nonetheless become the victim of a very strong and very sick man. Coral's insights help us understand how a girl stays in the incestuous relationship. Coral did not know she had a choice. She lived in a world where her father's word was *the* word. She coped by learning to numb her body so that she could barely feel the sex.

The special place Coral created in her mind, with its elaborate characters playing out intricate roles, saved her. She made them so real that they helped her live through the parallel reality of being forced to be her father's "lover" for six years. Also, because she spent so many summers in her early years at her paternal grandmother's home with her cousins, she had a sense of being loved. Sometimes having just one person reach out with love to a girl can pull her through her trauma. Girls find all sorts of ways to survive incest. Some leave their bodies; others catalog plants in their head; some even develop a totally separate personality during the molestation. These are all survival strategies.

Coral is still with the same boyfriend. They now live together. They have been together for five years, and for the first time in her life, Coral is able to enjoy sex as a normal part of a romantic relationship, as an expression of love. But trusting her boyfriend and standing up for herself in the relationship are still big issues for her. Because she never learned to trust, there is some tension, and Coral still struggles to identify her pure sensibilities and to weed out her father's influence.

She also works on poetry that tells her story. She conducts workshops at high schools. She is committed to reaching out to girls and helping them speak their truths. She hopes that her own truth has touched you in some way that will help you to triumph.

As a girl, when she wasn't being molested, Coral hung out with her friends and got into music and art. Garnet, another incest survivor, got into some pretty destructive behaviors after the molestation ended. She started smoking a lot of pot and cutting her arms, and she isolated herself from her friends. Garnet thought that all this would help her forget about her father molesting her, and it almost did—until he began to molest her sister.

Garnet

Garnet came to see me when she was nineteen. She was having trouble sleeping because she was afraid that her father, who had molested her over a period of time many years earlier, was now molesting her younger sister. The experience of her own molestation was also coming back to haunt her.

She had spent some of her young teen years cutting herself, and her parents and teachers never knew. By the age of sixteen, she had a pretty serious drug and drinking problem. She'd been in a few bad relationships, had had bouts of serious depression, and had always felt the shadow of her father's abuse. By the time I met Garnet, she had begun to settle down. She was teaching two art classes to young children and was going to college. She was working hard in her courses and at the teaching, which she really liked. But when she began to suspect that her father was abusing her younger sister and confronted him, he denied it. He denied molesting her sister, and he denied molesting Garnet. He told her that she was imagining things, and that she needed help.

She came to therapy to try to get some sense of what to do for her sister. Why didn't she go to her mother? Because she didn't trust her mother and was afraid that she would permanently reject her. In fact, by the time she wrote this story, she had told her mother and confronted her father, and they had both betrayed her.

{ *Garnet's Story* }
My Worry Spot

I was brought up on the Upper West Side of Manhattan. From the outside, my family looked oh so respectable. My mom is a high school guidance counselor, and my dad is a lawyer. We are Jewish, and when I was a kid, we went to temple every Friday night. We looked like the perfect family: close and connected. But behind closed doors, we barely spoke.

There are two kids in my family. I'm the oldest. My little sister is seven years younger than I am. Right before my adolescence, when my sister was a little kid, my dad started molesting me, and this went on for years. During adolescence, I got really depressed and started cutting myself. No one knew why—and they didn't even really seem to care. The few times my mom clued in to my depression, she just sort of brushed it off and said stuff like, "Oh, whatever it is you're going through, it will pass. Teens always get stressed out." You see, for a couple of years my dad and I had been acting as if nothing sexual had ever happened between us. I thought I could just forget about it and move on.

My dad first molested me when I was around nine. I remember the first time it happened. We were watching wrestling on TV. My dad and I were sitting on this big easy chair. The fireplace jutted out of the wall, and there was a space between the fireplace and the wall. We moved the chair closer to the TV into that little niche in the wall.

My father put his hand around the top of my jeans. I thought, "This is weird." Then he started to touch me. He groped around inside my underpants. I pushed his hand away, and he put my hand under his butt and sat on it. I pretended nothing was happening, and that I was just watching the wrestling. You see, my dad had always paid a lot of attention to me. He would take me hiking, he helped me with my homework, stuff like that. My mom was pretty checked out and never gave me much attention or showed much affection. My father was silent. He was putting his fingers in and around my vagina, and it really hurt. I do remember that, feeling the physical pain and then just watching the wrestling. (Needless to say, to this day I cannot watch wrestling. I have to go to the bathroom and vomit if I see it for no more than a moment when the channels are changing.)

It's hard for me to explain how I just let him do this to me. Sure, it is crazy to have your dad put his hands into your underwear, and I even surprised myself by not doing anything, but there was this odd combination of trust and fear and shame and terror that I did not want to deal with, so I actually pretended it wasn't happening.

After that incident, my father was all nice to me again. For about two weeks, everything was normal, and I tried to pretend it had never happened. Then one night, my father came into my bedroom. I had a very high bunk bed, and he asked me to come down. I said no, I was tired, and he started climbing up the ladder. I'd tried to kid myself that I had forgotten all about the other incident, but obviously I had not. I got this creepy feeling all over and gave the ladder a shove. He fell onto his back. When he stood up again he said with a sick grin, "What's the matter, Garnet? Daddy just wants to kiss you goodnight."

I was so scared. He told me that I was Daddy's princess, and that he would never hurt me. He asked me to please make him happy. Then he climbed into my bed and started to fondle me. He told me that this was the right thing, that it was time that I learned about men, that he would teach me what I needed to know. This felt really weird for about a minute, and then I blocked out the feeling and began to recite childhood hand-clapping games in my head *"Miss Mary Mac Mac Mac, all dressed in black black black, with silver buttons buttons buttons, all down her back back back, she asked her mother mother mother, for fifty cents cents cents, to see the elephants elephants, elephants, jumped over the fence fence fence, they jumped so high high high, they reached the sky sky sky, and they never came back back back, till the fourth of July -ly -ly . . . Miss Mary Mac Mac Mac"*. And then he was gone. I pulled up my panties and fell asleep.

My mother was involved in a lot of educational committees at the school she worked at, and many evenings my father stayed home and took care of me and my baby sister. Those were the nights I ended up in my father's bed. It's so strange. I don't even know how I got in there. It was like I was in a fog. He'd laugh this sick laugh and call out for me, and the next thing I knew, my wrists were being tied to the bedposts of my parents' bed with this ugly pale purple scarf. It was one of those cheap ones from a 99-cent store. (I know that scarf is still in the house.) He always put a pillow over my head, too. He didn't want to see me or for me to see him.

I remember the first time he tied me up. All of a sudden, his mouth was there. I remember thinking, *this feels weird,* but I just pretended water had gotten down there. I was just going into puberty. What the hell did I know? At first I thought, I'll be okay, I'll be okay, but then I realized how totally gross this was, and I was desperate to focus on something else. Of course, it was always really hard to focus on anything with that pillow over my face; it was easier when my face wasn't covered. I would try to pretend that I was floating in a fog, seeing beautiful colors.

He molested me in other parts of the house, too, and in the car; and he almost always kept my back to him. That made it easier for me, too. I could focus out the window of the car or at the TV.

One time we were in his room, and he had me tied up with the purple scarf and the pillow was in front of my face, when I felt something heavy drop on my chest. It felt slimy and hard, and heavy, and I was like, *oh my god,* and I started squirming around until the pillow came off my face. That was when I saw my father's erect penis on my chest. It was huge and hideous. A drop of his semen had fallen onto this one little spot on my chest. I freaked out and started screaming, but he didn't stop. He just put the pillow back over my face and continued molesting me.

After that night, I started scrubbing that spot obsessively to try to clean myself. Sometimes I'd scrub it until I bled. I would have to put Band-Aids on it. Even now, the spot seems permanently bruised and red. Whenever I am really nervous or scared about anything, I still rub that little spot on my chest. I call it my worry spot.

I tried to talk to my mom while all this was going on. I'd plead with her to take me to her meetings at night. But she said she counted on me to help my dad take care of my sister. When I told her that "Daddy tells me to keep secrets," and asked if I could tell her, she said, "If they are secrets, then you'd better not. You know you're Daddy's princess."

I felt so isolated. I mean, my mom was nice to me and all; in fact, she was just nice enough to me for me to think she loved me. She didn't yell at me much; we went to temple together; she made my lunch for school. But I never felt my mom was ever really listening to me, and I learned early on that the way to be accepted in my family was not to rock the boat. I was a good, compliant child. I always wanted to be closer to her, but I was afraid that if I tried, I would get turned away.

From the ages of ten to fourteen, the molestation continued. I was a good girl and did my schoolwork, played with my friends, and loved my cats. I remember the comfort of my cats and loving to snuggle with them and talk to them. No matter what, they always accepted me. I tried to have a good time in between the molestations.

Then, when I turned fourteen, something strange happened. My dad lost interest in me. My breasts had started to develop, and I got my period, and suddenly he stopped coming around. That year felt like a vacation, but there was always the fear that he might start up with me again. I became very anxious and depressed, and I started smoking cigarettes, then pot. My mom wasn't tuned in, and I began to really go downhill in school.

When I was fifteen, I finally confronted my father. I told him that I was messed up and that I needed to talk about the sexual abuse, and he said, "Abuse? By whom?" I was shocked. I said, "By you!" And he said, "Oh, Garnet, do not even think about destroying this family. Everyone knows what a vivid imagination you have. Who do you think they'll believe? You or me? Plus, I know all about the pot you've been smoking. I can report you." He actually threatened to turn me in!

That was when I started cutting my arms. When I'd cut, I was the one in control. It was like, *If I hurt myself first, no one else can hurt me.* The problem was, there was no feeling, no pain—only blood. But seeing the blood felt oddly comforting. It was tangible proof that I was alive, and I guess I needed to know that.

It's so weird about my mom. Here she was, Mrs. Big in the community. She had lots of friends and was always helping girls at her high school deal with abortions and family problems and stuff. She even stood up to my father on certain issues. For example, she maintained her Democratic political beliefs, and my father is a hardcore Republican. But nothing I did ever got my mother's attention. She always seemed oblivious to what was going on with me and my dad. She didn't even notice when I started cutting my arms.

I've always wondered how she couldn't have known about my dad. I told her many times that I didn't want to be alone with him, and I remember always wishing she would figure it out or walk in when my dad had me tied up. But she never did. My mom likes things status quo. If everything looks okay, then it *is* okay. I tried to bring up the abuse with her a few times, but somehow I knew she would choose my dad. Not that they got along great or anything, but she certainly wouldn't have wanted that mess on her hands. I just tried to bury the memories by getting stoned a lot and hanging out with my friends. I went from an A student to a C or D student. Even though it's been a few years since my father stopped molesting me, I certainly didn't feel good about myself. I would escape any way I could. When I was stoned, I would fool around with boys; it didn't matter what they did to me. Things had become pretty unbearable at home. But every year that my father didn't molest me, I began to feel a little bit better. Eventually, toward the end of high school, I realized that I would have to improve in school in order to get into college and out of their house, so I started focusing on academics and joined the drama crew at school. I stopped drinking and drugging and cutting, but I still hated being around my parents and was having bad dreams. At least I was able to push down the memories more effectively. When I graduated high school, my parents wouldn't pay for an out-of-state college, so I enrolled in school in another borough of New York City and moved in with one of my girlfriends and her family.

After I moved out, I kept in touch with my little sister, who was ten when I left. One day, I went to my parents' house to pick up something. They weren't expecting me or anything; I just showed up. When I got to the top of the stairs, I could see into my sister's bedroom. I could see my dad's back and my sister struggling to pull up her pants and put on her shirt. My father bolted out of her room and headed for the bathroom. I freaked out. I was shaking all over. I grabbed my sister and said, "What just happened with Daddy?" She pulled away from me and said, "Nothing! Why are you acting so weird?" Her eyes were kind of dead, like she was in a trance or something.

It had been four or five years since he'd touched me, but all the pain just came roaring back. I saw myself as a little girl, and I couldn't stop shaking. When my father came out of the bathroom, he very matter of factly said, "Hey Garnet, what's up?" That's when I became determined to stop him.

I started therapy with Patti because I had to save my sister, and someone told me she worked with abuse survivors. Patti told me that we would have to call child welfare to report the abuse of my sister, but first, we could call my mother in for a session. I was so scared. More than anything, I wanted to bust this open and have my mother finally deal with it. So we called my mother in, and my therapist helped me tell her what had happened to me and what I was sure was going on with my sister. Initially, my mother actually believed me. That really surprised me. She held my hand and cried. She even revealed to me that she had been molested by an uncle when she was a little girl. I told her about the sick purple scarf my dad had used with me, and she admitted that he had tied her up with that scarf, too. She cried and she held me. I couldn't even remember the last time my mom had held me like that.

When my mother went home and confronted my father, of course he flatly, and I mean flatly, denied everything. He said that I had a vivid imagination. He said that he believed that I believed it, but that of course it was not true. He started going on about my drug use, and about how sometimes drugs can increase the imagination. That's when my world really came tumbling down. My mother called me and told me what my dad had told her, and she ended the conversation with, "Garnet, I believe that you believe this, but it cannot be true. Why would your dad lie?" I tried to give her details to convince her, but she ended up taking my dad's side.

Then where was I? I had opened up the can of worms that my father had warned me not to. I continued to live at my friend's house, but I never told her anything about my family problems. I started going to Dr. Patti's sexual-abuse survivors' group, and I felt a lot of support from the other girls. It was the first time I realized you could never tell from appearances who had been abused. The girls in the group were beautiful girls.

They were smart and nice and cool. It made me think, "Wow, I wonder who else I know has gone through something like me?"

Meanwhile my father was interviewed by child welfare, and of course he portrayed me as a drug user and troubled adolescent. I was no longer allowed to go home, and my mother wouldn't even let me take my favorite cat. The child-welfare services people decided against prosecuting my father. They said there was no physical proof, and that because my sister didn't back up my accusations, they couldn't proceed. They described my father as decent and a good parent. Ha.

My father actually had the nerve to call me a few times to say I should drop everything. Then he called me on my birthday and said that I would always be his love. He said that he and I know it is all true, but that he will never admit it, so I should just tell everyone it's a lie. Then he started calling me three times a week and pleading with me to say that I had made it all up. He said not to worry, and that he would forgive me. His calls only made me more angry. I told him that if he kept calling me, he would have to talk to my lawyer. The calls stopped, but candy was delivered to my door on Valentine's Day with a card saying I should give up the lie, and that he still loves me.

Until I spoke about my abuse, I had this strange fear inside me, that somehow he still had power over me because I was keeping his secret. But now my father has no power over me. I'm an adult, and no one can force me to do anything I don't want to do. Now, with the support of my therapist, the group, and a few close friends, I am beginning to reclaim my life. I am working part-time and have taken out student loans for school. My parents don't financially support me anymore, and I wouldn't want them to. I still have bad dreams, I still freak out sometimes when I am touched in a certain way, and I still get depressed at times, but I do feel better. I don't feel the need to escape with smoking pot; I don't want to cut myself; I am basically learning to live with myself and have stopped blaming myself for all that has happened. I feel like this incredible weight has been lifted from me—the weight of my father's psyche, the weight of his body, the weight of his secret.

I am taking back my childhood bit by bit. It feels for the first time in my life like I am free. My worry spot is a reminder, but I can rub my worry spot and know that no one will violate me ever again, so I still rub it when I'm feeling freaked out. But now I tell my body that we will be all right.

My Thoughts

Garnet was incredibly brave and loving of her sister. She took a lot of risks. She may not have been able to disclose her own abuse while it was happening, but, as many girls do, she told in order to protect her sister. By reporting her abuse she took the risk of breaking up her family. She knew that her family might turn on her and deny the abuse, but she felt that no matter what the immediate outcome, her little sister would know, somewhere inside, however deep, that Garnet had tried to protect her.

In the short run, her worst fears came true. Her father played out his threat, and her sister lied, and she lost her family. She still struggles with this loss. She lost contact with her sister, who ran away from home at the age of fifteen. Eight years after Garnet reported the abuse, Garnet's sister called her. Through her sobs, she told Garnet what she already knew—that their father *had* been molesting her, and that that was why she ran away. Her sister admitted she was prostituting and a drug addict. She called Garnet to thank her for trying to help and promised that she would be in touch.

Garnet still holds out the hope that one day her sister, who is now eighteen, will show up on her doorstep.

Meanwhile, Garnet will always have her worry spot to remind her of her pain—and her triumph.

Life after Incest

I've worked with many girls who thought they could never be whole again because they were incest survivors, and I've seen so many come through this horrible ordeal, as Coral and Garnet both did. The beginning of getting through incest is simply knowing it was not your fault, not one bit of it. You are not alone. Wounds do heal. If you were the victim of incest, you may always feel the remnants of a scar, but you will not always feel the tremendous ache of a gaping wound. Incest survivors do get beyond their incest to lead happy, wonderful lives. They can have healthy, intimate sexual relationships. As you have seen in Coral and Garnet's stories, and will see throughout this book, the human spirit has a strength that cannot be crushed, even in the face of the most violating abuse.

There Are Ways Out

If you are still living at home, there are things you can do to protect yourself. You may not be ready to face the consequences that might result from telling your mother, but no matter how young you are and how dependent you are on your parents for housing and support, there are many other things you can do.

First of all, I want you to realize that through each positive decision you have made in your life—joining the debate team, playing the guitar, taking up acting, playing soccer, picking up this book—you made the choice to live your life, and please remember, it *is* your life. With each positive step you take, you are healing some of the pain your molester inflicted on you. One young woman once told me, "My father thought he had me; he thought I was his, but I was only lost. Now I am myself, and he cannot touch me."

Second, incest is against the law. We do recommend that you report it. This is not to say that reporting holds no risks. The authorities will check out your situation, and it is usually your word against your perpetrator's. If you live with the perpetrator, he may be removed from the home—or you may be. In the meantime:

* Try to find someone you can trust and start talking about it.

* Stay away from your father (or perpetrator) as much as possible.

❊ If you see any weakness in your perpetrator, you can try to threaten him with calling the police.

❊ If you are pretty sure he won't harm you, try to tell him no. Believe it or not, this sometimes works; more often, of course, it doesn't.

❊ Find a family member or friend to take you in.

❊ Spend more time away from home.

❊ Sleep over at friends' houses. I have known girls who've lived at a friend's home during their senior year of high school.

❊ Find some way to support yourself financially.

❊ Do as well as you can in school so that you have a good chance of earning a scholarship to college to get away from your molester.

Do what you can to keep him away from you. Girls do all sorts of things in anticipation of their fathers sneaking into their bedrooms at night. Some girls talk about wearing layers of clothing to bed to frustrate their fathers' efforts.

Even if none of these suggestions work for you, please know that what you are feeling—whatever it may be—is normal, and that one day, you *will* be able to get away. For now, you can go to our Resource Center to find lots of websites, supportive services, and other outlets to help you cope.

When someone forces you into an incest relationship, he borrows something precious from you—and very unkindly. Just remember: He can't take it forever. Your body, your spirit, and your heart are yours and only yours, and if you start to process your sexual abuse now, you *will* get them back.

Chapter 7

Too Close for Comfort
Other Incest–Brothers, Cousins, Uncles, Stepfathers

"heart jumping

body shivering

fingers clutching

zippers unzipping

sanity escaping

good-bye little girl . . ."

—A SIXTEEN-YEAR-OLD SIBLING-ABUSE SURVIVOR

Of course, incest doesn't happen only between fathers and daughters. Many girls are sexually molested by their brothers, uncles, and cousins. The wound may be different from, and the betrayal perhaps not as deep as, when a father or stepfather is the abuser, but abuse within families is always traumatic, no matter who perpetrates it.

Brother-Sister Incest

Brother-sister incest is one of the most complicated of all forms of sexual abuse. The statistics on it come primarily from the foster-care system. In fact, Mary Walker, a specialist on the foster-care system for thirty years, has observed in her work that as many as 90 percent of kids in foster care report having been sexually abused. We have better data on these kids because they are in the system, and because when a foster child is permanently adopted and displays strange behavior, such as overt masturbation or fear of being touched, the adoptive parents will usually seek services to help them—such as social work or therapy—and uncover the prior abuse. But it is impossible for us to know how widespread either biological or stepsibling incest is, since what goes on in private families often stays private unless someone comes forward to report it. And given the shame and secrecy that surrounds incest, that just doesn't happen too often.

What we do know is that brothers (and sometimes sisters) do sometimes sexually abuse their usually younger siblings, and that many of you reading this book will have had this experience. This chapter is for you. (While foster-care abuse is obviously a very important issue, this book is focused on invisible girls, girls whose stories aren't being told, so we'll be examining biological and stepsibling abuse. You can refer to the Resource Center for information on abuse in foster care.)

First, let's define terms. Sibling sexual abuse means any inappropriate touching or other sexual behavior between siblings. Being fondled; having your private parts touched or being forced to touch someone else's; being made to watch someone masturbate; being penetrated; being asked to view pornographic materials; being repeatedly walked in on in the bathroom or bedroom—these are all forms of sexual abuse. Any child over six can be an abuser; the abused can be as young as two or three.

Sometimes sibling abuse goes on for years. In his book *Sibling Abuse,* Vernon Wiehe devotes a short chapter to sexual abuse—short, in part, because reliable information is so hard to come by. As Wiehe points out, tracking emotional and physical abuse between siblings is far easier than tracking sexual abuse. Sexual abuse between siblings is usually kept hidden, either because there's so much shame or because there's confusion about what it is and why it is allowed to go on.

Just as with father-daughter incest, in families where there is sibling incest, there is always some problem with weak parenting. Girls will often say they didn't have the necessary closeness with a parent to tell them what was happening. You may occasionally hear about a single incident when a brother tried to molest his sister but got caught and punished. Sure, that happens—but it's rare. Often, there's a long pattern of sibling sexual abuse within the home, and the parents are either oblivious or dismissive. And girls are left feeling totally trapped and confused.

Many older girls feel tremendous guilt and shame about "letting" their brothers "get away with it"; younger girls will tend to have more fears. In all cases, it is safe to say that the parents weren't present in some important way.

Topaz

I met Topaz when she was sixteen. Her aunt brought us together. I was speaking about incest and sex abuse at a local high school when one of the social workers approached me to tell me about her niece. She began to sob as she spoke of the guilt she felt about not protecting her niece from her nephew. "Why couldn't I see it?" she choked out, tears streaming down her face. She went on to explain that her niece had just been released from a two-month hospitalization for a suicide attempt by overdose. During her stay, she had revealed that she had been sexually abused by her older brother for four years.

As I would later discover in sessions with Topaz, the abuse began when she was ten. She and her brother lived alone with their mother in an affluent New York suburb. Their mother worked long hours in Manhattan and was rarely around. They were Italian American. Both children attended private school and were good students, although John, Topaz's brother, had started getting into trouble for cutting classes in junior high. When he hit high school, he started drinking and staying out late. Most of the time, he seemed to be seething inside.

Topaz, by contrast, was sweet and outgoing. She was on the debate team at school, was very social, and had many girlfriends. Topaz was the type of girl you could count on. She could keep her friends' secrets, she could always be counted on to partner for school projects, and she came through for friends, teachers, and family.

One day after school, when she was fifteen, Topaz came home and swallowed what remained of a bottle of Tylenol. As she began to fall asleep, she realized she did not want to die. She managed to get to the phone to call her best friend and told her what she had done. Her best friend and her best friend's mom raced over and took Topaz to the emergency room. The hospital contacted Topaz's mom, and she showed up at the hospital within the hour. That's when Pandora's box burst open.

{ *Topaz's Story* }

Brotherly Love Gone Bad

I am sixteen years old and have been in therapy (with Patti) for about a year. For a while, I could keep everything together, at least on the outside, but then I crashed. I think that crash saved my life. Pretty ironic that it took an overdose to save me.

My brother and I live in a very affluent area of Westchester County, New York. Our parents got divorced when we were very young. We barely ever saw our dad when we were young, and now we never see him. He moved to London and has a new family. Our mom is something of a workaholic. She is an investment banker and keeps very long hours. My brother and I have always had au pairs or nannies taking care of us.

When my brother got to be a teenager, we all agreed that we could be on our own for the most part and no longer needed live-in help. So from then on—I was ten and he was about thirteen—we would only have babysitters from the time we got home from school until our mother came home at around 8:00 PM That's when things started to get weird with my brother. My mother's room is on the ground floor, and ours are upstairs. Once we would go up to bed, she would go into her home office and do more work. She had no idea what was going on.

My brother and I were very different. I always wanted to be perfect. I wanted to do really well in school, never make waves with my friends, and keep my mom happy. My brother and I never really talked about anything deep, but we did hang out a lot and played soccer together and talked about music. He was usually pissed off about something or at someone, but he was pretty nice to me. I think that's what was so confusing about the whole thing.

Now a bit about my mom. She has always been super-ambitious, but when she met my father, she decided to stop working and have kids. When my brother was little, she spent a lot of time with him, and then I was born when he was three. My mom continued to stay home with us until I turned three and my brother was six. That's when my father announced that he was moving out with his secretary. Because I was such a little kid, I really don't know much more about it than that. All I know is that my mother started working again, and my world changed. I realize now that my mother became much more emotionally remote when my father left; she wasn't there for me, even when she was home. I think it really wasn't her work so much as her depression.

I was really lonely and leaned on my brother for "kid" companionship. We had our babysitters, and they were nice, but I still felt lonely. My mother would work long hours and then come home and read or do more work-related projects, but she didn't really talk to us or spend any time with us. I was craving love and attention and affection at that time.

Once I got a little older and started doing really well in middle school, she started paying some attention to me. She liked to help me with my schoolwork and projects and would tell me how proud she was of my good grades. Even though we didn't talk about a lot of personal things or really connect, that was the only time I can remember my mother focusing on me. It wasn't predictable or anything, but I did enjoy it. Until high school, I was still very much a pleaser.

My brother was much more daring and independent. He always did well in school, but he wouldn't give my mom the time of day, especially as he got to be a teenager. He was always off either with his friends or playing soccer.

By the time I was a teenager, I started realizing how much my mom was not there for me, and I started to reject her. I was really pissed off. She did not fight it, and the three of us kind of led parallel lives. Except at night. That is when my brother and I would have sexual contact.

It all started when I was about ten. One day my brother, who was thirteen at the time, brought me over to the neighbor's to play soccer. Our neighbor was a very "cool" seventeen-year-old. His parents were never around, and as it turns out, he and my brother were hooking up, but I didn't know it at the time. They told me to come inside for some cookies, and then they both asked me to watch them play a game. Up to that point, I was having a great time. Well, it turned out that the game was that the neighbor would jerk off my brother, and then my brother would jerk him off. I froze—I was shocked and scared. I didn't know what to do. I sat there and ate my cookies and looked down, and I didn't say a word. I avoided the neighbor after that.

That night when I was in bed, my brother snuck into my room. He said, "Hey, what Adam and I did is really fun. I want to teach you how to do it, too." I told him I didn't want to, and that it kind of grossed me out. He said okay and left.

Then, about a week later, my mom and brother had a huge fight. He came into my room crying, and I felt really bad for him. He told me he felt really unloved and asked if he could just sleep in my bed with me. I said okay. I was a little nervous, but nothing happened. He actually did this a number of times over the next few months: just come in and sleep in my bed. My mom didn't seem to notice.

My brother really seemed sad and would tell me that I was the only one who really loved him. But he never touched me or anything. He also stopped hanging out with our neighbor. And I started liking the warmth of another body in my bed with me.

After about six months of this, things changed. One night I was dozing off, and I felt my brother begin to rub up against me. I did not know what was going on, but I just pretended to be asleep. He started doing more and more stuff to me, and I just kept pretending to be asleep. He put my hands on his crotch, and then he touched me. I knew it was wrong, but I didn't have anyone to talk to. My brother and I never talked about it, and I never told.

The weird thing is, it would go on for a few weeks, and then not for months, and then it would start up again. When I was about twelve, I hit puberty and got my period. This may sound really strange, but that's when I started to like how it felt when my brother touched me. We never had intercourse or anything, but we would touch each other in very sexual ways, and my body would feel really good. This was probably the most confusing time in my life. As much as my body was reacting, in my mind I knew it was gross; it was wrong, and yet I didn't stop it. I started to have irritable bowel syndrome, where I couldn't go to the bathroom for days on end. Now I realize it was because I was holding in so many of my feelings, but at the time, it just felt awful.

The stuff with my brother continued on and off for the next two years. Then one day, it just stopped. My brother got serious with a girlfriend, and he never came to me again. After a few months of my brother not approaching me, I actually started to relax a little, and my stomach problems were less intense.

When I was fifteen, he went off to college. That's when I started thinking about the incest a lot. I feared that what I had done was disgusting and wrong, and that somehow, everyone knew I had liked it. I felt terribly ashamed, but I really missed my brother. So I kept really busy. Honestly, I don't know how my mother couldn't have noticed that something was wrong.

I did try to have boyfriends. Of course, most of them just wanted to hook up without any relationship, but after what had happened with my brother, that felt natural to me. I just kept finding new boys to hook up with, and I started to get a strange reputation in my school. I was seen as this really nice girl and good student and not really a slut, but a girl who would not say no to guys.

Of course, no one knew how totally depressed I was. One day, I couldn't take it anymore and decided I wanted all my feelings to end, so I took a bottle of Tylenol. But once I started to feel drowsy, I got scared and called my best friend, whose mom I also really trusted. Thank goodness they were home. They took me to the hospital and my stomach was pumped. I was so tired from coming off the Tylenol that I didn't have the energy to lie, and when my best friend asked me why I had done it, I could not stop crying. I told her all about my brother sexually abusing me. I just spilled everything out. My mother, my aunt, and my best friend's mom were also all in the room, and everyone freaked out.

As soon as I told, I regretted it. I shut down and refused to talk about it anymore. But my mother made me see a counselor. I didn't want to talk about it, and I didn't trust the counselor, and things just got worse. I was so depressed that I stopped focusing on school and just slept a lot. Then I was hospitalized. They put me in a ward with other adolescents who had problems— eating disorders, depressions, sexual abuse—and I began to talk with other kids about what had happened.

The family therapist made my brother come to a session where I had to tell him how upset I was with him for doing what he'd done. It was in that session that my brother broke down and admitted that the neighbor had sexually abused him starting when he was about ten and the boy was thirteen. By the time my brother was twelve, it had become habitual. He said his abusing me was his way to get out and away from the neighbor. It really confused me seeing my brother break down like that. I was finally angry, and it felt good, but when my brother started crying, I actually felt sorry for him, and that put me in a strange place.

When I finally got out of the hospital, the kids at school had a lot of questions. It was really hard. My mother also got into therapy, and it came out that she had been abused by her uncle when she was a little girl and had never told anyone about it. She started to realize that a part of her was so terrified that I could be abused that she had just closed off her feelings. This is very sad, because it turns out that the cycle of abuse continued, both with my brother and with me.

Needless to say, there was a lot of pain around our house. My mother told me how sorry she was for not being a part of my life, but she continued to work long hours and still wasn't really there for me.

Then my aunt told me about a therapist she had heard speak at her school and about a group for survivors. I started therapy and joined the group, and that's what really began my healing. I was filled with shame and conflicting feelings, and I had to forgive myself big time. The group supported my anger toward my brother. I still can't really imagine ever forgiving my brother. I do not feel any pity for him. As a matter of fact, I'm still really pissed off at him. I am also really angry at my mom. The one person who really came through for me was my aunt. I moved in with her after the hospitalization, and that probably saved my life—at least my emotional life—because she told me again and again that it wasn't my fault, what happened with my brother. She reminded me that my brother and I were just confused and scared.

It's funny, because although my aunt was never all that in-volved in my family before, she feels the worst. She tells me over and over again how sorry she is that she didn't figure out what was happening and do something. I think she takes it es-pecially hard because she's a social worker who works with teens and thinks she should have known somehow. I know she feels really guilty, but I always ask her how she could have known. I remind her that I wore many masks: the good girl, the good student, the happy kid, the sister who loved her brother. It's that last mask that still confuses me the most.

My Thoughts

Topaz was a very lonely kid. Her mom wasn't around much, and her brother was her only real companion. She was comforted by having him sleep next to her in a home where she felt little closeness and comfort from adults. We can actually see a lot of parallels between Topaz, Coral, and Garnet's stories. Like Topaz, both Coral and Garnet wanted their mothers' support but never got it. We know that Topaz and Garnet's mothers suffered abuse. These mothers weren't close enough to their daughters to intuit the abuse. And Topaz's mother was ignorant of what was happening, not only with her daughter, but also with her son. All three girls were left on their own at a critical time.

Of course, we also see how sexual abuse and incest cycle through families. It turns out that Topaz's brother felt deeply rejected by his father's leaving. Then, when his mother started working after having been pretty accessible to him during the first six years of his life, the feeling of rejection and aloneness intensified. When he was just ten years old, his thirteen-year-old neighbor started paying attention to him, and he craved that attention. Too bad the attention was sexual and inappropriate. Topaz's brother revealed in family therapy that the neighbor was also being abused—by his coach. Her brother wanted to break away from the abuser but did not know how. Plus, he continued to get something important from the connection that he wasn't getting anywhere else. It's a pattern we see often: Many boys who are abused turn around and abuse someone else.

In family therapy, Topaz's brother talked about how, as an adolescent, he was terrified of being gay, and he was afraid of girls, so his sister seemed like his least threatening choice. When a girl his age finally showed some interest in him, he no longer needed to sexualize his sister.

The thing that was so confusing for Topaz was that she enjoyed the physical sensations, and that made her ambivalent about stopping him and ashamed when she didn't. The fact is, our bodies are conditioned to respond to sexual touch. But most important to note is that in most incest situations, the abuser sweetens up the abuser first, and this is precisely what Topaz's brother did. By coming to her crying, by wanting to cuddle with and sleep with her, especially when she, too, was feeling vulnerable and lonely, he gained her trust. This was very confusing. Because Topaz was such a pleaser, she felt sorry for her brother and wanted to make things okay. But it wasn't okay. Her brother knew how and where to touch her to arouse her, and she felt confused by her body. Girls of this age will often say they felt "deceived" by their bodies. No matter how they might be feeling—angry, upset, sad—their bodies are still aroused. That's why girls who have been abused will often hook up with lots of other boys—just for some of those familiar feelings of being touched. Another reason sexual abuse survivors may hook up with boys is to feel some power or that they think that's all they're worth. That's what they've been taught.

Once again, it's striking how lack of maternal support can be so damaging to a girl. Their mother never figured out what was going on. But there's no real surprise there, either. Siblings often have a pretty easy time keeping secrets from their parents, especially if their parents are themselves hiding an incest secret. It seems amazing that people can live in such a state of denial, but it happens all the time. As we discussed earlier, often the mother is in a dysfunctional relationship herself and can't face what's going on, or feels powerless to do anything about it.

A girl recently wrote to my website:

> "When I was twelve and my brother was sixteen, he used to come up to me and squeeze my breasts. He thought this was the funniest thing in the world, that my breasts were growing. I was mortified. When I told my mom, she told him to stop, but he never did, and she never pressed the issue. Now that I am fourteen I hate to be touched by anyone. I am jumpy, especially around boys. I always feel as if someone is going to come up and grab my chest. Was this sexual abuse?"

Of course it was sexual abuse! Many girls get confused when there's no genital contact, but any unwanted pinch of the butt or chest is sexual abuse, especially if it is allowed to go on without punishment (to the perpetrator), and it can be very distressing to girls who are entering adolescence.

Sage

Sage's molester didn't live in her home. He was an older cousin. Unfortunately, he was often left alone to take care of Sage, and her parents were too busy to notice that anything was wrong. He started molesting Sage when she was eleven. She liked having him around because he paid attention to her. They played cards, they ordered pizza for dinner, they played video games. The abuse actually seemed a reasonable price to pay—at least for a while. When she was around thirteen, she started getting more creeped out by it and told her mother. To her mother's credit, she forbade the cousin from ever setting foot in the house again. But unfortunately, her parents never brought it up again and remained aloof as she was growing up.

I first met Sage when she was seventeen and a friend brought her to one of my sex-abuse survivors' groups. She had just disclosed her abuse to a friend, and that friend knew she'd need support. We worked together throughout her senior year of high school, but when she turned eighteen, her parents threw her out of the house and told her to fend for herself. Because they'd never really provided even the basics for her, she wasn't all that surprised, but she needed to figure out how to survive.

When she went for an interview to waitress in a topless club and was offered work as a topless dancer instead, she decided to do it because the money was so much better. She says she didn't really feel any shame or embarrassment about dancing topless. She'd learned many years earlier, she says, that feelings were dangerous; they led only to disappointment. She had learned very early on how to shut down her feelings and practically numb herself to the world. Her body may have been dancing, but her mind and her spirit were always somewhere else.

Sage's story not only gives us a glimpse into the world of women who dance topless but confirms what we have been saying about male-dominated culture and its objectification of young women. It shows how an unsupportive family, sexual abuse, and a culture that views girls as sex objects can compel a girl to feel she is good for only one thing: her sex appeal.

{ *Sage's Story* }

My Family Threw Me Out

I am nineteen years old and a survivor of child molestation. From the ages of about eleven to thirteen, I was made to do things that most kids don't begin to learn about until much later. In fact, the perpetrator was in his early twenties himself. He was twenty-three and my cousin. He was a really nice guy, friendly, good-looking—and he was really fun to be around. But sometimes he would force me to participate in oral sex, masturbation, and passionate kissing. I can remember him exposing his genitals to me and touching my private parts as well.

Looking back, I think I didn't tell right away because I didn't want him to stop coming over. That may sound sick, but you know, at least Jack paid attention to me. My parents were very young, and they were very involved with each other and partying with their friends. I always felt like I was a bother to them. Jack was always over at the house, and when other people were around, he played with me. He'd teach me card games, throw around a ball with me, and play Frisbee with me.

When I was thirteen, I finally told my mom the truth about what Jack would do to me when he came over, and she told him never to set foot in the house again. She also told me to stop flirting and walking around in skimpy shorts. It's weird, but I kind of missed him. I didn't like how he pushed me sexually, but I did like having him around. At least he was around, which is more than I can say for my parents. For a very long time, I was afraid of boys and relationships. I still have never had a boyfriend, and I actually still have never kissed a boy. So you will be surprised when I tell you that I danced topless for a year at a club.

Of course, I can't blame Jack alone for my becoming a topless dancer. My parents had a large part in everything, too. And the money was really good. When I graduated from high school, my parents told me to move out and support myself. I shared an apartment with three other girls and was teaching children dance at a weekend program and taking courses during the week. I had a student loan and was a part-time college student, but I knew I couldn't make it through school without a better-paying job, so I started looking for full-time work. I heard you could get great tips as a waitress at this topless club near my apartment. When I went in to interview for a waitressing job, the woman managing the club asked me if I would be interested in topless dancing instead. It had never occurred to me. She told me I could make three times as much money if I danced, and that I shouldn't worry about being unsafe. No one was allowed to touch the dancers. That's how I became a topless dancer at the age of eighteen: to put myself through college. I did it for about a year.

Almost all of the girls and women I worked with at the club had been sexually molested as young girls. No kidding. I know because they told me so. And they all came from families that were totally unsupportive of them. Let's just say most of us did not feel particularly loved growing up.

Let me tell you what it felt like to be a topless dancer. It may sound strange, but in some way it built my self-esteem. On slower nights, I'd stand in front of a guy and dance. That's called a table dance. As I danced, I would think, "Should I give him a $40 dance or only a $10 dance?" That felt like a lot of power. I knew how to get them to pay. I'd add up my money as I danced. I even enjoyed making them feel small and stupid. They'd ask me if I had a boyfriend, and I'd say, "No, but if I did, it certainly wouldn't be you!"

It didn't gross me out to dance. I saved $10,000 in one year to pay for college, rent, bills, etc., and I just kept my life and my work totally separate. I never went out with customers. Never. Sometimes when I'd go home after a shift and snuggle with my cats and drink hot cocoa, I'd think, "I don't believe what I did today. I danced naked." But mostly, I can't say I had many feelings about anything at the time. I knew I wanted to go to school and pay my bills and not depend on my parents for anything, because they were unreliable. I knew I had no power in my family, but as a dancer, I did have power.

Just think of the symbolism. There I was, standing above these guys. I was looking down, and they were looking up to me. These bankers, lawyers, doctors—all they wanted was to talk with a beautiful young woman. They'd show me pictures of their kids, talk about their jobs, or ask about me. If I could keep them talking, I didn't even have to dance. Some nights I made several hundred dollars just talking to these men.

But I could also be really mean. I'd be witty and sarcastic and tell these men they could die wanting me because I would never be with them. I even smacked a few of them who tried to touch me. If a customer tried to touch my nipples, I'd rip his hands off me and say, "You're not a very fast learner. Now sit on your hands!" I guess it's as if everything I couldn't say to my cousin as a kid came out with my customers.

There was one weird thing about it, though. I could always tell who was a pedophile. You see, I have a body like a little girl's. I am very petite. When Jack molested me, I was barely developed. And if a customer would watch me in a certain way, I could almost feel his pedophilia. I can't explain how, but I just knew. When I had to dance for a pedophile, I'd get really nauseous. No amount of denial would work. I'd freak out and have to take a break.

I quit after a year, when I began to realize what a heavy price I was paying for the money. I was letting men use me as a fantasy object, and it started to get to me. After a while, I would look out into the audience and envision the men as animals screaming and trying to touch us—all these young, scarred girls.

Dancing definitely changed me. One of the changes is very obvious. I used to wear more revealing clothing: tight shirts, hip-hugger jeans with a short shirt to show off my pierced belly button. Now I wear overalls most of the time, or baggy jeans.

Recently, I told my mother that I'd been a topless dancer. She didn't seem shocked or anything; she just said I should be careful, and to watch out for illegal behavior. She didn't really seem to care. And she actually said she would like to try it sometime.

I know I'll have a lot of emotional consequences from that work, but I don't want you to have a prejudice against topless dancers. I am not a prostitute, and many of the girls would never be with a customer. The girls who do have sex with customers are almost all abuse survivors who don't feel they're worth better. But they're not bad people.

It's still really difficult for me to get in touch with my feelings. But with Patti's help, I filled out college student loan applications, and I just received a student loan and some financial aid. I'm beginning to sort things out and to feel better about myself. Maybe all that dancing was my way of trying to dance out some of my pain.

My Thoughts

Of course, most girls who experience incest don't become topless dancers, but it makes sense that many dancers were molested as girls. They know how to disassociate. Sage used to disassociate the entire time on her job. She only tuned in when she felt her body being violated by a customer. Then she'd respond by either angrily removing his hand or yelling. It was a challenge working with Sage, because during our time together, she was still dancing in the club. This was hard for me, because I could see what a great person she was and knew there was a part of her that felt violated by her job, but she couldn't quit. One day she admitted to herself and to me that she felt trapped and confused, just like when she was younger and molested by her cousin. She was ready to stop shedding her clothes and start shedding her guilt, and that was the day she was finally able to quit. Again, girls may take some detours to their healing, but have faith. You can always come back.

※ ※ ※

If you are a survivor of incest with a cousin, brother, or uncle, please know you are probably keeping one of the best-kept secrets of all abuse. It is not your fault. You are not dirty, and you are not guilty. If you can, call a hotline, tell your abuser to stop, lock your door, or confide in a trusted relative.

I have worked with many girls who have survived incest and moved on with their lives. I will tell you that some of them never did forgive their brothers or their cousins or their uncles, and some of that anger actually empowered them to move forward. You do not have to take this from anyone, not even your relatives.

Chapter 8

Trusting the Wrong Men

Abuse by Teachers, Coaches, Clergy

"I kept getting better and better at tennis, and everyone was
excited for me. What they didn't know was that my coach was
having sex with me after our practices."

—A SEVENTEEN-YEAR-OLD SURVIVOR OF MENTOR ABUSE

If you've opened up any major newspaper in the last five years, you've
probably seen a headline like this: "Teacher Arrested for Molesting Student"
or "Teenager Molested in Principal's Office." In New York City in 1999,
the assistant principal of Stuyvesant High School, one of the top high
schools in the country, landed himself on the front page of the newspaper.
The photograph showed him handcuffed and being taken away by the
police. It turns out that this sixty-plus-year-old man had been soliciting
sexual favors from a fifteen-year-old female Asian student who volun-
teered in his office in the hopes of getting a slot in one of the school's
highly coveted biology programs. Another recent case that made headlines
involved a forty-plus-year-old teacher taking his sixteen-year-old student
across state lines to marry her. Cut to 2003: The headmaster of a prominent
New York City private school is arrested for downloading kiddie porn
on the school computers.

Sexual abuse isn't something that happens only in families. Many girls
are lured or even forced into having sex with older mentors, such as priests,
rabbis, teachers, coaches, etc., sometimes in exchange for favorable treatment,
sometimes out of infatuation, sometimes entirely against their will. The men
usually who have some power over the girls' lives and who use their power
to coerce the girls into crossing appropriate boundaries.

We have already seen how susceptible to pressure adolescent girls can be. And in Chapter 3, we looked at how having an unsupportive family can make you vulnerable to abuse. So it makes sense that sometimes a girl will fall prey to the manipulation of a man with great influence in her life—and often a very positive influence, as in the case of a coach, teacher, or clergyperson. It can be all too easy to fall under his control. You like the attention of your coach, for example. It's very flattering and makes you feel special. But is it okay if he puts his arms around you to "console" you when you're alone in his office? Is it okay if he asks to kiss you? Is it okay to sleep with him if he tells you he loves you?

Of course, there's a big difference between the kind of encouraging warmth coaches may exhibit—from an arm around your shoulder after you missed a play to a hug after a defeat—and sexual abuse. For instance, however annoying it may be, a coach who is weight obsessed and hounds you to lose a few pounds and gain muscle in certain areas of your body to improve your ability at a sport is not sexually abusing you. However, if he laughs and stares at your breasts bouncing up and down as you shoot for a basket, or even if he makes lewd comments but never touches you, that is sexual harassment, and it's not okay. Suffice to say that if you are feeling uncomfortable about the attentions of a teacher, clergyman, or coach, it's okay to question the behavior, to say stop, or to get help from someone you trust. If you're confused about the difference between inappropriateness and abuse, you can flip back to Chapter 1 for clarification.

Mentor abuse is also all bound up with our male-dominated culture's obsession with youth and beauty. Remember Lolita? Apparently, many men find adolescent girls "irresistible." They think that when we're in our sports uniforms or dressed up for church or trying out new teenage fashions, we're "asking for it." A girl sticking chewing gum on her leg for an audition (see story about the director of the *Lolita* remake, Adrian Lyne, in Chapter 2) can somehow turn into "a seductress" in the mind of an abusive man.

Just listen to what Cardinal Francis George of Chicago had to say during the meeting of U.S. cardinals with Pope John Paul II in April 2002: "There is a difference between a moral monster like [the Rev. John] Geoghan [who engaged in sex with boys] and someone who perhaps under the influence of alcohol engages with a sixteen- or seventeen-year-old young woman who returns his affection."

Talk about a Lolita complex! Don't you know tons of young women who want to sleep with their priests? Aren't all girls just "returning their affections" or "asking for it?" And just think of all those poor, hapless men who can't help themselves! Right?

The fact is, some men in positions of power will misuse that power through sexual abuse. As far as we know, it has been going on since the beginning of human history, and it happens all over the world. But that doesn't mean it's okay, or that you have to go along with it.

> "When I would go home at night, I would busy myself, distract myself, organize something, make sure I did not have time and space to really think about what my coach was doing."
>
> —A NINETEEN-YEAR-OLD MENTOR-ABUSE SURVIVOR

The biggest difference between incest and sexual abuse by a mentor is that in this case, you actually get to go home after the molestation. You do not have to live under the same roof as your abuser, and the sense of violation and shattered trust is not so primal as it is with a parent. But, like any form of sexual abuse, mentor abuse is a huge violation of trust and often leaves girls feeling very unsure about how to form healthy intimate relationships.

In this chapter, we'll look at how abusive mentors tend to work, first gaining a girl's trust—and often, especially in the case of clergy, the trust of her parents and family—and then making their way toward a sexual advance. Of course, the abuse is not always premeditated. Some men just lose their sense of boundaries and get carried away. But it's still abuse, and it's still not okay. An older man and a teenage girl cannot have a healthy sexual relationship, no matter how mature she may be or how much it feels like love. There's just too much power in his hands and not nearly enough in hers. Period.

In the case of mentor abuse, there are many different types of predators. We'll hear a variety of short takes in this chapter and read some letters to my website from girls who were abused by their teachers, coaches, rabbis, priests, chorus teachers, professors, and tutors. Too many girls have kept these secrets. It's time we lifted the taboo.

Before we hear from the girls, let's stop and take a look at some of the most prevalent myths about mentor abuse:

MYTH: Pedophile priests are only interested in boys.

TRUTH: The media may have jumped on the story of sexual abuse of boys within the church, but the truth is that, as with all forms of sexual abuse, far more girls than boys are the victims of sexual abuse by clergy—ministes, priest, rabbis. In fact, according to Mary A. Tolbert, professor of biblical studies at the Pacific School of Religion, girls are three times more likely to be molested by clergy than boys. She suggests that a combination of a profound fear of homosexuality and a devaluing of girls is what leads our society to be scandalized by the abuse of boys and turn a blind eye to the abuse of girls. A. W. Sipe, a former Catholic priest and psychologist who studied sexuality in the Catholic priesthood for twenty-five years, estimated to the *Boston Globe* that "more than twice as many priests are involved with females as with males."

Of course, in our male-dominated society, the greatest public outcry is reserved for abuse of boys. When girls are abused, we tend to shake our heads and *tsk-tsk*; when boys are abused, we are outraged and want justice. And if these boys turn out to be homosexuals? Our culture says that would be a high crime.

The truth is, clergypeople can and do sexually abuse children, and their targets are predominantly girls.

MYTH: It's against the law for priests to molest minors.

TRUTH: Clergy are often exempt from laws governing conduct, and the church has always protected its priests against public exposure or criminal charges by moving them from parish to parish. It is very difficult to get the government involved in cases involving clergy, although things are beginning to change.[1]

MYTH: If your priest or other religious or spiritual leader is molesting you, it must be all right in the eyes of God.

TRUTH: Of course this is not true. Sexual abuse is always wrong, no matter what your priest might tell you.

MYTH: Clergy can't be sexual deviants, predators, or pedophiles. They are pure and holy, called by God to be leaders within their communities.

TRUTH: People enter the clergy for all kinds of reasons, and just as in the general population, some clergy are emotionally unstable and prone to sexual abuse. As the recent scandal within the Catholic Church would suggest, priests are just as capable of abuse as anyone else.

MYTH: Male preschool and elementary school teachers are attracted to the field for predatory reasons.

TRUTH: This is another instance of society's gender prejudices: After all, what kind of man would honestly be interested in teaching and nurturing young children? The truth is, most of the sexual abuse that goes on in schools is between male teachers and teenage girls.

MYTH: You have to do what your coach tells you to do.

TRUTH: Coaches sometimes exploit their position of power. You never have to have sex with a coach or let him touch you in a sexual way.

MYTH: It's sometimes necessary, as part of the training, for your coach to get a little "fresh" with you.

TRUTH: As we said in the opening to this chapter, if a coach harasses you a bit about losing weight, that's not sexual abuse, although it also might not be true or appropriate. If he stares a little too long when you run, that's harassment, even sexual harassment—but it's not sexual abuse. But if he touches your breasts or even just makes sexually loaded remarks, that's abuse, and you can report him.

Ivy

Now let's meet Ivy, an Orthodox Jewish girl who was molested by her rabbi when she was fifteen. I didn't meet Ivy until she was twenty-one. She was going to college in New York City and one of her friends, a client of mine, brought her to see me. At that point, Ivy no longer had much contact with her parents. She described her relationship with her family as "superficial."

She was supporting herself and paying for college with student loans and had stopped observing Judaism, having become suspicious of all rabbis and of religion in general. This is pretty common in cases of clergy abuse: Girls will tend to generalize their bad experiences to include all clergy and all religion.

Ivy thought she had pretty much put the abuse behind her, but then, six years after her molestation, she started having nightmares and developed a case of irritable bowel syndrome.

{ *Ivy's Story* }

I Tried to Forget

My family was very religiously observant and went to synagogue regularly. My parents were very close to the rabbi and his family. In fact, my best friend growing up was the rabbi's daughter, Sara. We all lived in a small Jewish enclave in Borough Park, Brooklyn, and I would often sleep over at Sara's house. Sara was like a cousin to me, and she would come to my house often as well. We went to camp together, we were classmates, and we shared secrets. Sara did not seem close to her father, who was usually working at the synagogue, and because he was so religious, he seemed to be observing one Jewish holiday or another, and was not around much when I was at Sara's house.

One night, when I was about fifteen, I was sleeping over at Sara's. Sara was already asleep when I heard footsteps approaching her room. When I looked up, the rabbi was standing over my bed. He looked at me and whispered "*sha*" ("be quiet" in Hebrew). He was very quiet and sat down next to me on the bed and started petting my hair. I was so nervous, I pretended to fall asleep, hoping that would make him leave.

Before I knew it, he was lying down next to me and rubbing up against me and fondling my breasts. I froze. I prayed he wouldn't notice that I was awake. I began counting to ten over and over again and keeping track of how many times I'd done it. By the time I had counted to ten about twenty-five times, the rabbi had gotten up and left. I just lay there in shock.

I could not sleep and just lay there awake until morning. Sara, on the other hand, appeared to sleep through the whole thing. When we woke up the next morning and Sara asked what I wanted for breakfast, I made up an excuse not to stay for breakfast, and I ran home.

When I got home I told my parents right away what had happened. They did not believe me. They said I must have been dreaming, that our wonderful rabbi was not a "pervert" and wouldn't have done these things. They said I should be ashamed of myself for such an accusation. They then marched me over to the rabbi's house, forcing me to tell my "story" to him. Of course, the rabbi denied everything.

Now comes the twist. Sara must have been listening at the door, because she suddenly burst into the room and confronted her father about how he had molested her for years. In front of me and my family, Sara broke into sobs, saying that she'd been terrified to tell anyone, but that she wasn't going to let him get away with molesting her friend, too. Can you believe the adults didn't believe us, even with Sara there crying and everything? My parents just looked at their beloved rabbi and said, "Rabbi, how could this be?"

In the face of overwhelming evidence, the rabbi continued to deny that he had ever touched either of us. At that point, Sara, who was usually so mild mannered, began to weep uncontrollably. And that's when Sara's father lost his cool and started screaming at Sara violently. It became clear, even to my parents, that there must have been some truth to what Sara and I were saying.

I went over to Sara and hugged her, and she fell into my arms. I kept saying, over and over, "I am so sorry, I didn't know." Suddenly, my one night with her father seemed like nothing in comparison to what he'd done all these years to my dear friend, who had been hiding it the whole time.

My family took me home and broke off all relations with the rabbi and the synagogue. When I would see Sara in the hallways at school, she'd avoid me. My parents forbade me to go over to her house, and she did not even want to walk home from school with me. My family felt shame for me and asked me not to tell anyone. They finally said they believed me, but they didn't want to talk about it. After a few months, the rabbi's family moved to Israel, and I never heard from Sara again. I also never told anyone about Sara or her father or what he did to me. I just buried the experience deep down inside. I became more isolated. I did not trust anyone. I certainly couldn't count on my parents, so I just kind of withdrew into myself.

When I graduated high school, I moved out and enrolled in college. I limited contact with my family. But six years after this incident, I started having nightmares and becoming depressed. That is when my friend brought me to therapy."

My Thoughts

When Ivy came to see me, she made it clear that she didn't want to talk about what had happened with the rabbi as much as about how her parents had not believed her. That's what had hurt the most. Her parents had kept it a secret all these years. When Ivy once approached her mother to talk about the abuse, her mother said, "Look, it only happened once. Put it behind you." This is a very common experience for girls. When you are abused "only" once, most people don't understand why you are upset. But one traumatic experience can upset you for years.

If Ivy had been able to process the abuse and keep in touch with Sara, she might have worked through it by the time we met. But she had already experienced six years of repression by then. What Ivy discovered, as do so many other girls, is that there is often lots of unfinished business, even for the survivor who discloses her abuse.

As she described it, the experience had made Ivy very suspicious of religion and of men in positions of power. She had a very hard time trusting her teachers and problems being intimate with men. Through her therapy, she began to give herself credit for having taken care of herself by opening up about the abuse. The more we worked on rebuilding her confidence in herself, the more she was able to open up to others. She realized that she really had done the right thing by telling and could trust herself to take care of herself.

The creepy experience with the rabbi, coupled with her parents not believing her, had caused her to build a wall around herself. But slowly she realized that the wall stemmed from not trusting herself, and that by getting in touch with how brave she had been to tell, she was able to regain that trust and let other people in.

Of course, after six years of rape, as in Coral's case (see Chapter 6), a girl will have some very heavy and complicated feelings and symptoms to deal with, but all girls who are sexually abused share some common feelings of shame and mistrust, which can sometimes last for years. Many girls who are abused once or twice feel guilty about even having feelings about it, because they know other girls have had it much worse. But I am here to tell you that even "just" once is once too many! It's not at all unusual to develop emotional problems from just one abuse experience. You have a right to your feelings. And that doesn't diminish anyone else's right to theirs.

In the continual flow of letters to my website, probably one out of five has to do with some kind of mentor sexual abuse. Often, girls start out feeling flattered by the attention of their mentors. There can be a kind of natural intimacy between an adolescent girl or young woman and her coach or teacher, especially when a girl is particularly successful and excited by the sport or subject. For example, having your high school English teacher encourage you to submit poetry for publication, or a coach invite you to try out for a varsity team, can be really exhilarating, even life-changing—particularly if you are already feeling vulnerable and/or don't have a good relationship with your father.

Other factors make some girls more vulnerable than others. For example, it may be a part of your cultural tradition to obey your elders, no matter what. Perhaps females have a very low standing in your culture. Girls who are experiencing other traumas—their parents' divorce or a death in the family, when all the adults are focused elsewhere—might be more susceptible to sexual abuse by a trusted mentor. Girls who are going through depression might be particularly seducible by a coach who says he can guarantee her happiness. It's easy, then, to project onto your mentor certain protective or parental qualities or to be overwhelmed with gratitude. That is why girls often feel so confused and guilty over mentor abuse. But make no mistake: These men are manipulators wearing the costumes of supporters.

Also, if you were molested as a young child and never told anyone because you felt unsafe in your family, for instance, you might be more susceptible to mentor abuse. But if you were molested early on and told somebody and got support and results, chances are, your sense of boundaries will be better developed. You know that people support you and believe you, and you'd probably be better at spotting the warning signs (he looks at you a little too longingly, he hangs around a little too often, he invites you out for coffee, etc.). If you are uncomfortable and unsure of your mentor's vibe or intentions, talk about it with a trusted adult.

One girl wrote to my website for help with her confusion about her coach's inappropriate advances:

> Dear Dr. Patti,
>
> I live in Tucson, Arizona, and I am a freshman in high school. I read the other letters on your website and had to write to you. I have never told anyone about this, but something really weird happened to me with my basketball coach. He is no longer working at my school, and I have not seen him since he left, but I've been so scared to tell anyone what happened. I am scared that he will come back and find me and say I am lying.
>
> He used to work with me privately and tell me how great I was. He is only in his early twenties and very good-looking. I admit I liked the attention. But one day while we were shooting baskets, he tackled me to the ground and stuck his tongue in my mouth and

put his hands up my shirt. I just lay there. I feel so stupid about this now, but I was really freaked out and didn't know what to do. I kept playing basketball after that, but I never stayed after or spent any time alone with him again. It was just that one time. I thought I was over it, but now I am having nightmares. Was I sexually abused? Was it my fault? Should I tell?

—*Suzanne*

Yes, Suzanne was sexually abused. No, it was not her fault. She did not know her coach would tongue-kiss her or forcibly touch her breasts. Many girls talk about this kind of thing happening just one time, after which they avoid the person. This is often the best thing to do. It's even better to find a trusted adult to tell. The adult can help you figure out what to do next, and can also help you deal with the feelings that come up so that you aren't scarred with fears and mistrust.

Another girl who wrote to my website had a "relationship" with her mentor that started out "nicely" but became abusive over time:

Dear Dr. Patti,

I am twenty years old and just finished my second year of college in the Midwest. I recently ended an "affair" with my eleventh-grade English teacher. I always felt special in Mr. X's classes. I come from a family of overachievers whom I could never measure up to, but he told me I was really smart. He also told me that he loved me, and that age did not matter (he's thirty-four). I knew he was married, but he always said his wife didn't understand him and I was the only one who did. He wrote me poetry and bought me gifts, and I was very flattered by all the attention.

The affair started with us going out for coffee after school. By the middle of my senior year, we were getting together sometimes on the weekends. He would take me to poetry readings and stuff. He said that his wife knew but was never around for him, so it didn't matter. My parents thought it was a little strange that this teacher spent so much time with me, but they liked him, so they didn't seem to mind much. He would stop in and chat with them, and I think they just thought he was a great guy.

Then one Saturday after coffee he took me to a park and told me he was falling in love with me. He said he wanted to kiss me and asked me if it was all right. I said okay. I remember it was a strange feeling, sort of like kissing some old guy from TV or something, someone you watch but would never want to get intimate with.

By the end of my senior year, we were spending a lot of time together. That was the same year my parents got divorced and my father moved out. Mr. X really came through for me then. My mother was depressed, and I barely even saw my father, with whom I already had a strained relationship. I told Mr. X everything and really leaned on him for emotional support. He was great. He even called my mother and told her not to worry about me, that he'd keep an eye on me.

Slowly, he convinced me to stop seeing most of my friends so we'd have more time together. When I went away to college, he visited me, and that's when we had sex. I didn't want to lose him, so I complied. I also thought he was the only person who would ever love me that much. But after the first time, I didn't want to do it again. It just felt creepy. But when I said I didn't want to, he got really angry and forced himself on me, saying he had given up his marriage and moved out and was in love with me. I later found out that none of that was true. I began to get frightened, and I wanted to break away, but he was very controlling, and I was afraid of what he could do to me. I was afraid he'd tell my parents and they'd freak out. I stopped eating. I became depressed. I didn't want to see Mr. X anymore.

I went to the counseling center at my school and told a counselor about the relationship. She told me it was not consensual and that it amounted to sexual abuse. She also said that she would speak with Mr. X and tell him to stop contacting me or she would report him.

To make a long story short, I told Mr. X what the counselor said, and at first he was very angry, but then the weirdest thing happened. He broke down and cried and admitted that he had been with teen girls for ten years. When I told my counselor that, she totally flipped out. She told me to threaten to take him to court if he did not seek help. I was kind of scared of the whole mess and let her contact him. She made sure he got into therapy.

I feel like a coward. I should probably report him so he won't molest other teen girls, but I don't have the courage. I feel so guilty and dirty. Even though my therapist tells me it was not my fault, I feel like I asked for this relationship. Reading the other stories on your website, I see that other girls have forgiven themselves. Why can't I forgive myself?

—Mary

Mary had a really traumatic experience. She was forced into a romanticized, sexualized relationship with her teacher, a teacher she really liked but didn't want to have a sexual relationship with. Just as pedophiles look for vulnerable children who are alone and unsupervised, sexual-deviant mentors will look for girls who seem somehow unprotected and vulnerable.

Mary did not have a strong relationship with her father and barely saw him after he divorced her mother during her senior year. When Mary started to confide in Mr. X, sharing her vulnerability and her sadness, he perhaps surmised that she would be more open to his "comfort." The boundaries in these situations get very confusing. Mentor abuse is very painful, just as incest is, because often the girl really looks up to and trusts the person who then turns around and sexualizes and abuses her. It only confuses matters if the family also knows and trusts the mentor.

Also, let us be aware that all around us—in films and advertising and magazines and other media—the idea that very young women are attracted to older men is thoroughly normalized. Even in the TV series *Gilmore Girls*, the otherwise outspoken, assertive, brilliant girl character Paris goes off to Yale and has an affair with her sixty-plus-year-old professor. We know from earlier episodes that Paris is desperate for the attention she can never get from her parents. Of course, girls are always blaming themselves for the situations they land in. But look around you. Look at the culture—specifically at movies—and you easily see how girls are constantly being set up for these "romantic" liaisons with older and oh-so-much-wiser men.

If you are a survivor of mentor abuse or are currently involved with a mentor, please understand that these relationships are not okay, even if they are encouraged all around you. Even if you've been told that it's perfectly normal, that the age difference means nothing, that you're an "old soul" or were connected in a past life, and even if this is a relationship that you don't feel hurt by, you must trust me that you will be hurt by it at some point in your life, because at its root this kind of relationship is all about power.

No matter how "mature" you are or how "ready" you feel, as a teenager you are simply not on an equal footing with an older mentor. Once you are twenty-five or so and have matured into adulthood, it is entirely up to you to decide whom you become intimate with. But, as a teenager, having a relationship with a much older mentor is a whole different story.

To those of you who might currently be involved with a mentor in a sexual relationship, please know that it is best for you to end the relationship as soon as you can. I urge you to take to heart everything we've said in this chapter. Do not blame yourself. It's not your fault, and it's never too late to change your situation.

Often, threatening to report your abuser is enough to stop him. Chances are, you are not the first girl this man has taken advantage of, and mentors are all too often terrified of being exposed or investigated because they know how long the list of their other "affairs" is.

Although things are slow to change, there are laws protecting girls against sexual predators, and it's worth checking the laws in your state. As you'll read in the date rape chapter (Chapter 10), many universities across the nation have created sexual assault prevention and awareness training programs for students and faculty.

Justice is rarely served in cases of mentor abuse, but you always have the power to walk away. Remember: Your mentor may be charming and flattering and give you the attention you crave, but the wonderful talents he is offering to nurture in you are *yours*. He did not create them, and you do not owe him sex in exchange for his kindness. If you are attracted to him, remember that your relationship is not a partnership of equals and never will be.

It may be painful and confusing in the short run to refuse the advances of your mentor, but trust me: You won't regret it.

Chapter 9

Pushed Too Far Too Young

Acquaintance Sexual Abuse

"I felt as if I was sinking into a drain. I had nothing holding
me up, nothing keeping me afloat. I watched from the
sidelines as he touched me."

—A FOURTEEN-YEAR-OLD ACQUAINTANCE-ABUSE SURVIVOR

Acquaintance abuse differs from date rape in that, by definition, you already know the abuser before he rapes you, and it may not involve going on a date at all. In fact, you may not even be dating yet. You may be twelve years old. "Tweens" and young teenage girls are particularly vulnerable to acquaintance sexual abuse. You may be friends with the guy or know him from around the neighborhood. You may even be attracted to him, but instead of taking it slow with you and exploring in a way that you can handle, he takes advantage of your confusion and vulnerability and pushes you much farther sexually than you are ready to go.

Myths and Truths about Acquaintance Abuse

Here are some of the most common myths and misunderstandings about young adolescent girls and their sexuality. And to counter these myths, here are some of the truths I have learned from the hundreds of girls and young women I have spoken to through the years.

MYTH: Young teenage girls have enormous sexual appetites.

TRUTH: Given how complicated puberty is, a statement like this is simply ridiculous, and yet it is widely believed. Here's the truth: Some girls feel arousal, and some do not. Many twelve-year-old girls start becoming interested in boys (or girls). They may want to kiss, but they do not necessarily want their genitals touched, or to touch someone else's. They have all sorts of thoughts and feelings and lots of fears of the actual sex connection. They are not emotionally ready for consummation of sexual physical contact, and this is the essence of what abuse is—a girl not being ready emotionally to integrate what she may be experiencing physically.

That's where boys and men get confused. A thirteen-year-old girl may dress like Britney Spears and be attracted to and intrigued by boys, but *that doesn't mean she wants to have sex with them.* She may have posters of Justin Timberlake on her wall and have romantic fantasies about him, but in reality, she doesn't want a teenage boy, no matter how cute he may be, putting his fingers in her vagina. Usually a girl's true sexual appetite begins at around age fifteen.

Around the age of fifteen or sixteen, a girl is cognitively, emotionally, physically, and spiritually ready for deeper relationships, including sexual ones. This is a time when most girls have completed their tasks of emotionally separating and reuniting with their parents and have the mental equipment to manage a relationship that is both emotionally and sexually complex.

MYTH: Young girls enjoy giving boys blow jobs.

TRUTH: There is a great deal of pressure out there for girls to perform oral sex on boys. Nowadays blow jobs are thought of as casually as kissing in much of teen culture. Sometimes giving a blow job is even a rite of passage into a peer group. But underneath the bravado is fear—and even disgust—on the part of the girls. In all my years of working with girls, I cannot remember ever hearing a twelve- to fifteen-year-old say she enjoyed giving boys blow jobs. In fact, a girl that age can experience mild to severe physical discomfort, such as gagging, choking, and nausea, if she tries to perform oral sex. Many girls have gagged when forced to swallow semen. It can also cause real emotional turmoil. Most girls just aren't ready.

MYTH: Twelve- to fifteen-year-old girls are in command of their sexual appeal and deliberately use it to manipulate boys. They feel sexy, beautiful, and powerful, and want to turn guys on.

TRUTH: Twelve- to fifteen-year-old girls usually feel gawky, awkward, ugly, and embarrassed by their developing bodies. No matter how they appear to others, they hardly feel sexually attractive. They're busy adjusting to all the changes and mourning some of the losses that come with developing hips and breasts and getting their first menstrual periods. They are navigating new waters, figuring out how to deal with their new bodies and hormonal surges.

At this developmental stage, girls naturally feel confused by their sudden "sex appeal." They may be pushed hard to start experimenting with sex and to conform their emerging sexuality to cultural expectations. They may start to wear makeup and experiment with dressing in a more sexy way, and they may seem to become women overnight, but few girls are truly "in command" of their sexuality even at fifteen—let alone twelve, thirteen, or fourteen.

MYTH: Intercourse feels great at this age.

TRUTH: Intercourse at this age usually hurts and is usually scary. It's simply not something that most twelve- to fifteen-year-old girls desire at this stage in their physical and emotional development, no matter how much they may want attention from boys. Of course, there are the rare cases when two young people really feel in love and ready for this commitment, but this is very unusual. I can't tell you how many times girls who have had intercourse too early (by their own reckoning) have told me that they could not understand the point of it. They say things like, "It hurts. You bleed. Sometimes you even have a hard time walking the next day."

Any girl brought up in a household where she didn't feel valued as a person, where she wasn't supported when she tried to create clear physical boundaries, where she didn't feel vital or important, where she felt invisible, is vulnerable to acquaintance sexual abuse.

Remember Coral talking about feeling proud and pretty in her new little outfit? She also said that after being raped by her father, she felt dirty. The rape took away all her comfort and pride in her developing body. It's hard enough just to deal with the feelings that come up during adolescence, but when a girl is sexually assaulted, as Coral was, she'll tend to close off her feelings. The same kind of thing happened to Amber, whom you'll meet in a moment, when she was forced into a sexual relationship too early. As Amber moved through all the normal developmental stages of adolescence—wanting to fit in, feeling awkward and uncomfortable with her changing body, feeling confused about her "sex appeal"—she didn't have a solid base of support at home. She felt lost at sea with all these new feelings. Along came a good-looking, popular boy, and she succumbed.

Amber

I met Amber one day when I was speaking to a large group of girls at her school. I remember looking at her and seeing a kind of dazed expression on her face. After the talk, she approached me and told me that some things had happened to her that she had never told anyone. We spoke that day for at least an hour.

Amber told me she was haunted by some weird experiences she'd had with a male counselor at her riding camp a few years earlier. She said he was a really popular guy at camp, and no one knew that he'd molested her. She explained that now she goes out with boys when she doesn't even like them and is confused about how much attention she seems to need from them. She knew it had something to do with the boy who molested her. She harbored a lot of resentment toward him but also felt guilty because she hadn't stopped him. She was obviously in a real state of emotional turmoil.

Amber described how angry she felt all the time, and how she carried her anger into her classes, into her relationship with her parents, and into her relationships with both girls and boys. Although she spoke in a monotone, as do many survivors when they are revealing their abuse for the first time, even in that first encounter I could see her body begin to relax.

Shortly thereafter, Amber started coming to my office, and over the next few sessions, she filled in the details of what had happened. The molestation took place over two summers, when she was twelve and thirteen. Her anger was palpable. During sessions she would often clench her fists.

We started our work together in the spring of Amber's sophomore year in high school. She was involved with the poetry club at school and was a good student, but did not derive much joy from her academic success. She had had trouble connecting with boys and with girls and described her quiet and conservative parents as well meaning but incompetent in many ways. Slowly but surely, it became apparent that Amber had a lot of reasons to be mistrustful.

Amber was African American. An only child, she lived with her parents and grandparents, who seemed "pretty clueless" about modern teenagers. Amber's father ran a small dry cleaning company and was rarely home, so Amber spent a lot of time with her mother and grandmother. There was no real openness in Amber's home, and furthermore, there was an expectation of blind respect for elders. It was assumed that Amber would be a "good girl," which included being kind and thoughtful to her elderly grandmother, a bitter woman who herself had lived through some very rough times during the Depression in the South.

Amber had no doubt that she was very loved by her family, but she felt that she needed to play a role to please them. If she acted out, she was always quickly reprimanded by her frightened mother, who was still under the thumb of her own mother. She got the message loud and clear: Don't make waves.

When Amber began her "tweens," she wanted to fit in but wasn't at all sure how.

{ *Amber's Story* }

He Told Me I Was Special

I have been holding in this secret of sexual abuse for years. I have never told my parents or reported this person, but when Patti came to my school, it all came back to me, and I had to tell the story of what happened.

I am African American and an only child. My skin is very light. My grandmother on my father's side is also very light skinned. This is a positive thing in my family, to be light skinned, but it is very uncomfortable for me because I don't really fit in anywhere— not with the interracial kids, the black kids, or the white kids.

I have always known my parents love me, but I could never really be open with them. We live in Staten Island, New York. This is a community with some very wealthy people and some working- and middle-class people, but it is not very integrated. I am not sure why my parents moved to such a white neighborhood, but they did. My family is middle-class; my father owns a small dry cleaning company.

When I was twelve years old, I was already pretty physically developed and felt really awkward. Boys started looking at me differently, and men on the street would whistle. People thought I was at least fifteen. My mother and grandmother both had huge breasts, and I had always prayed that I would not turn out like them. I remember I used to slump my shoulders to try to hide my breasts. This was the same year that I discovered riding horses. When I was on a horse, I felt great. I wasn't self-conscious. I didn't care what anybody thought. I just had a good time.

I started going to the stables near my house after school pretty much every day, and finally my parents scraped up the money to pay for some riding lessons and the tuition for the summer camp at the stables. I didn't have a lot of friends in school, and I noticed at the stables that there was a popular group of girls from my school. There I was with my kinky black hair, different skin, and thick body. All the popular girls seemed to be pretty and blond and rich. Once again, I didn't fit in.

That summer at riding camp, that same group of blond, pretty, popular girls were also there, but they talked to me very little. There were some black kids there, but they pretty much ignored me, and I felt kind of isolated. Then Tim came along.

Tim was sixteen and a really good rider. He was also very good-looking, and whenever he could, he showed off his six-pack. He was black and seemed to have crossed the popularity barrier. He was popular with all the kids. Whenever he rode to the stable, all the kids got excited; they thought he was so cool.

He worked part-time at the camp and was friends with all the kids. Because I did gymnastics I was really strong, and Tim noticed. I felt great when he asked me to be on his volleyball team and his team in water tag. This was my ticket to acceptance. All the kids knew that Tim included me on his teams.

Suddenly, different girls were asking me to their houses. I was really happy. I started to feel really good about myself and accepted by a popular group for the first time. This was the first time I felt as if I was actually "in" a group. Girls were calling me, and I could feel free to call them. Whenever Tim was around at camp, everyone surrounded him, but he would always talk with me the most.

One day when we were all at the beach, Tim was rubbing sand off my back and touched my chest. I felt kind of weird, but I didn't say anything. I figured it was a mistake. After that, Tim started paying a lot of attention to me. He would compliment me on how strong I was and constantly praise me during volleyball or water tag games. I felt really special. My parents could see how happy I was, and they were really pleased with all my new friends. Things were good.

One night, there was a campfire at the camp, and when everyone was sitting close together in the dark, Tim started whispering things to me. He said things like, "Bright Eyes, you know how special you are to me. Here, let's do something and don't worry about it. I really like you." Then he put my hand on top of his pants. I felt really weird. I was paralyzed and didn't know what to do. But he said, "It's okay. It's our secret." And he kept telling me how special I was. I knew it was probably not normal, and it felt weird, but I was hoping it would never happen again.

Things started to escalate with Tim. He would get me alone whenever he could. If I was alone with him in the stables, he would push me down on a haystack and fondle my breasts.

Then he'd take my hand forcibly and put it on his crotch. I'm sure I said no, but I'm also sure it was a pretty weak no. Really, I can't tell you exactly what I was thinking, because I would find something to focus on and just check out. After each of our encounters, he was really nice to me. He kept trying to get me alone, and I would try to avoid him. In the meantime, the girls were all being really nice to me, but they were always trying to get me to get Tim to come along to the park or the ice cream truck or something. Tim was clearly more interested in being alone with me, but he would come with the group sometimes. In retrospect, I now see that this was his way of keeping me hooked.

The summer ended, and I did not see Tim during the school year because he was away at boarding school. He actually wrote me a letter saying how special I was and how sorry he was if he had done anything to make me uncomfortable. He told me he loved me. I wrote back once or twice, but then we lost contact. I spent that year in middle school feeling accepted. I still didn't like my developing body, but I stayed active in sports and had lots of friends. I had almost blocked out Tim's weird touches when summer rolled around again—the summer before high school.

Sure enough, Tim showed up at camp that summer. At that point, I was fully developed and very curious about boys. I had a repulsion and fear about Tim, but also a strange excitement. My memories are blurry about this, but I have a sense that I actually wanted to be with him sometimes. I had this fantasy that he really loved me and maybe would be nice to me. But when he got me alone, all he wanted was to put my hand on his crotch. I would do it, and he would touch mine.

When we were alone together doing all this stuff, I would blank out or think about a movie or anything to get my mind off what was happening. One time he fingered me, and once he forced me to go down on him. I just pretended I was floating above my body, but I felt really awful afterward. Of course, I never told anyone about any of this. I did know I wanted to hold him and kiss him, but I did not want to do the other stuff.

The sexual stuff with Tim went on for the whole summer. I really can't explain why I was never able to stop him. It just became expected behavior from me. It wasn't until the end of that summer, at thirteen, that I finally told Tim to stop. Things had gone way too far. Even though I would blank out during the sexual encounters, I started having nightmares, and I also wanted to hurt myself. I cut my arms a couple of times with safety pins, and then I realized that it had to stop. When I told him that I wanted to tell someone, he said, "You know, you've let this happen a lot. No one will ever believe you if you say you didn't like it." Tim actually realized I meant business and was no longer going to go along with him, and he became really nasty. He either ignored me or was really sarcastic if he said anything to me at all.

The summer ended, and I started high school. I was in a new school with new kids. I felt horrible about myself. When I got really down, I continued to cut my arms with safety pins, and I began to smoke pot. I was repulsed by my own sexuality. I either wanted to feel pain or nothing at all. Much of my freshman year was spent inside a shell. I didn't want to make new friends, and I definitely didn't want to go out with boys. I basically buried myself in schoolwork. I'd come straight home after school or maybe hang out a little with the kids I bought pot from. I was lonely.

The summer after my freshman year, I took an accelerated writing course. Then tenth grade started, and I actually started to feel a bit better because I had had a good summer. No one had hurt me. But I was still really shy, insecure, and self-conscious, and I blamed myself for all my sexual encounters with Tim. I was not as self-destructive; at times I wanted to cut my arms, but I smoked pot instead and found myself just feeling angry most of the time.

Then one day, there was an assembly about sexual abuse. I went to that assembly, and it changed my life. That is when I met Patti and started to get counseling. I also started going to a survivors' group, and I realized I wasn't the only girl who'd been sexually abused. Some of the other girls who'd been abused felt the same way I did about boys. I was really afraid. I didn't want boys to touch me, and I definitely didn't want a boyfriend.

I still have a lot to deal with. I have so much anger at my parents. They're so weak. I am angry that they couldn't tell I was so depressed during my young adolescence. I'm really upset that I had to find counseling, that they never even suggested that I get help, and now I don't even tell them I go. Patti lets me pay $10 a session, and it makes me feel like it is my private way to heal and deal with my issues. My family is all about not making waves. They always want everything to be just fine.

Only now am I beginning to realize that I wasn't to blame, and that Tim probably did this to lots of other girls, too. For all I know, Tim may still be molesting girls, but I still don't feel strong enough to track him down and go to the authorities. One of the best things I've done, though, is that I've begun writing in a journal. My journal has become my friend. I wrote the following poem to that little twelve-year-old girl who couldn't stop someone from hurting her:

Hear the wind rush

feel the pain

ignore the chill

and hide the scars

count backwards from ten and pretend you're

somewhere else

where all the colors in the world become one.

Now it's over

he's leaving the room

I can breathe

at least until tomorrow . . .

Maybe then, though, I'll let myself see

that it's all up to me.

I'll clench my fists tightly

and tell the truth.

It was his fault, not mine.

My Thoughts

This was the first time Amber had told her whole story. She let herself go back to the beginning and track how and when it all started. She was able to share her confusion and shame about not stopping the sexual abuse. She talked about feeling guilty and lost and not knowing how to stop the boy from violating her. She believed her abuser when he told her that she must have liked the sexual fooling around, and that she obviously wanted him to do these things to her, but it's obvious to her now that she did not want to be sexually molested. She did not want to touch this boy's penis; it did not feel good to her. She was twelve years old. She felt insecure, awkward, and ashamed of her body. With Tim, she was pulled into a pattern, and she did not know how to stop it.

Because Amber did not have parents or friends she could trust, she didn't feel safe disclosing what had happened. Amber did what so many girls do: She pretended that she had forgotten. She tried unsuccessfully to suppress the memories of what happened and turned to hurting herself with safety pins. When that did not numb her, she smoked pot.

Through the accelerated English class, Amber was able to feel proud of herself again. She found some inner strength and really applied herself to her schoolwork. However, summers were hard for her; all the associations of the season—the smells, the heat—brought back memories of what had happened at camp.

In order to get through the abuse, Amber disassociated from her body. She described floating above her body, as if she was not participating in the encounters. There are even some blanks in her memory because she checked out so successfully. (This was mentioned as one of the brilliant things girls do to survive in Chapter 5.)

Many girls find ingenious ways like this to cope with their abuse. They feel trapped, and floating away or hovering above their bodies is how they survive. Disassociating helped Amber feel less "disgusting" about what happened. But it didn't stop her pain entirely. As we see so clearly in her story, before she told anyone, she was sitting on a volcano of feelings, which led to some pretty self-destructive behavior.

It's worth noticing that Amber knew Tim was bad news. She felt wrong about the encounters from the very beginning, but, like so many girls her age, she acted against her intuition. Her drive for social acceptance was stronger than her will to say no. Of course, sometimes saying no doesn't work anyway. But in many cases of acquaintance abuse, the guy is also going through some kind of adolescent angst. If you tell him no, he might become scared and stop. Of course, he also might become more insistent and threatening. It's impossible to predict. You have to trust your gut about whether it's safe to say no. But in all cases, it's best to find a trusted adult and tell. If the kid who abused you goes to your school, he might be forced to go to therapy, or he might even be expelled. You can petition for a legal order of protection, which would force him to stay a certain distance from you at all times. The point is, you have options.

As we saw in Amber's story, it took her a long time to tell anyone, and she has yet to tell her parents. She did not trust her parents to come through for her. Many girls won't go to their parents if they think their parents won't stand up for them. Again, you have to go with your instincts. Once Amber started talking about her abuse, she realized she was cutting her arms simply to feel something. She stopped smoking pot to self-medicate. She received a scholarship to a college out in California and feels ready for this new chapter in her life.

Jasmine

I met Jasmine when she was sixteen years old. She started coming to our sex-abuse survivors' group at her high school. For the first several meetings, she was very quiet. I knew she was Israeli, and I wondered about a language barrier. But then after a few group meetings, she spoke. Her English was perfect. Jasmine told the group she felt very guilty about taking up group time with her story because many of the girls had been molested by an uncle or father, and her molester was a boy back in Israel. She said she realized that most of the other girls were much younger than their molesters and had no power, but that her abuse was probably her fault because she should have known better.

Then she began to tell her story. Jasmine explained that she had been abused by her brother's friend and felt really guilty and confused about the abuse. He had forced her to give him blow jobs when she was thirteen, and now she was pretty promiscuous. She knew that she had a reputation for being a slut and felt like she deserved it. Sex, being taken advantage of by boys—this was familiar ground to Jasmine. But now she was beginning to realize how much guilt and shame she carried around. It was time to speak up.

{ *Jasmine's Story* }

The Boat

I moved to the United States when I was fourteen years old. I was born in Israel and was sexually molested there by my friend's brother when I was twelve. I already spoke some English when we moved here, so getting acclimated wasn't really all that hard. In fact, I'll be going to college next year—a year early.

I'd say I've always been pretty happy overall. I've always been a good student; I work part-time; I have some really close friends; I'm on the track team at school. But the abuse experience is always in the back of my mind, no matter what else is going on. The whole thing is still really confusing to me.

We used to spend summers in this small town near the beach. Down the way lived my friend Izhar. I was an only child, and Izhar, who was a year younger than me, was like a little brother. He had this cool older brother, Jakob, who didn't hang around the littler kids much, but I remember he would sometimes give us these special candies imported from the United States.

Izhar's parents had a big house. It was much more fun than ours, so we always hung out there. The summer I turned twelve, we were playing cards at Izhar's house one day when his brother came in and dared us to play strip poker. I was nervous, but I kind of liked him, so I said yes. I was down to my bra and jeans when I said, "That's enough!" His brother laughed at me, but he didn't push it.

Another time I was over and waiting for Izhar to come home from his guitar lesson, Jakob invited me into his room. All we did was sit and look through his CDs. But the next time he was alone with me, he asked if he could touch my hair, then my nose and my eyes. He said, "You are so pretty." Then he gave me a bag of those imported candies. Stuff like this went on for a while, I guess. I was nervous, but it was okay. He told me that even though I was two years younger than him, he really liked me.

Every girl in our town had a crush on Jakob, and I admit I loved the attention. But when he put his fingers down my underwear, I remember just kind of freaking out inside. I didn't want to scream or anything—that would have been too embarrassing—but I stared at this one painting on the wall. It was a painting of water and a boat. He fooled around with me like this a bunch of times, and I completely memorized everything about that painting—the colors, the boat, the places where the paint got thick and lumpy. I remember wanting to be in that painting. It was my escape.

I didn't say anything about what was happening with Izhar's brother to my parents. I think I didn't want to bother them. I was pretty close to my parents. My father had lost his job, and my mother was working two jobs to support us. I didn't think my problems with Jakob were really all that important. So I just tried to stay away from him. But I missed Izhar.

The next summer, when I was thirteen, Jakob and I played strip poker a lot, and I was pretty excited at seeing his naked chest. One time when the game was over, Jakob asked Izhar to run out and get us sodas. That's when Jakob opened his pants and took out his penis. He told me to suck him. I started to cry, and he pushed my shoulders down and put his penis in my mouth. I remember gagging and then vomiting all over the place, all over him, me, and my clothes. He pushed me away and yelled at me, saying I was a stupid girl who could not do anything right.

I ran home and was sick all night. After that I stayed away from Izhar's house for a long time. But eventually I went back again. I know it seems crazy that I would go back. Jakob apologized and said he wanted me to be his girlfriend. He said he wouldn't do that again. I told him I didn't want to be his girlfriend. He just shrugged and laughed.

A couple of weeks went by, and by now Jakob was ignoring me. But one day I was walking to their house through a path in the woods, and there he was. He told me he wanted me to give him a blow job. "It's nothing," he said. "You can do it without puking, you know." I was really scared. The look on his face was mean.

After that, he abused me once in a while, and mostly I stayed away from him. I was so confused. I still kind of liked him, but I hated how far he was pushing me, and I didn't know how to stop it. I remember how he would shove my shoulders however he wanted my head and mouth to go, and how I eventually learned to give him blow jobs and not gag. This went on for the rest of the year until I turned fourteen and we moved to the States.

I was happy to move away from Israel, and I thought I'd left all that behind me. The memories started flowing back, though, when I started attending Dr. Patti's groups. I mean, it's not like I ever forgot what happened or anything, but I started realizing that I was still hurting a lot from it. I am so grateful that I will never have to see Jakob again. When I think about what happened to me, I still feel disbelief. In Israel no one talked about anything like this.

After coming to the group for a while, I began to connect what happened back in Israel with some of my weird behavior around boys in the States. Like, I was seeing this guy right after we moved here, and he asked me to give him a blow job. I complied, but I did it in an almost robotic way. It was so weird. After that, I broke off the relationship. I was an honor student, always worried about grades, joining all the academic clubs, staying home weekends with my family, but I was not a "good girl" when it came to sex. I never had intercourse or anything, but I went a lot farther than I wanted to go. It was like I had this secret, separate, sexual life that was different from who I was in every other way.

When I was fifteen, I was with different boys. I knew they were using me, so I stopped seeing any boys for a while and spent some time alone. After I started going to the group and hearing the other girls talk, I realized that I did not have to be sexual with boys if I didn't want to be. I really did not want to be with boys. I realized that I wasn't to blame for what had happened with Jakob, and that just because that stuff happened didn't mean I had to let boys push me further than I was comfortable going.

Eventually, I got to know a boy from my school, and we became very close friends. After being close for a year, we started going out. We have been dating for six months now. We celebrated my eighteenth birthday together. It's the first healthy relationship I've ever had. He is a wonderful guy. He is also Israeli and has been in the States for about five years. When we got really close, I told him about the sexual abuse, and he was so supportive and loving. He did not make me feel dirty at all. He does not pressure me to have sex, and I still don't feel ready. He does these really sweet things for me; like on Valentine's Day, he snuck into school early and put this adorable stuffed teddy bear in my locker. He never forces anything on me, and he is very sensitive and gentle. But sometimes when he touches my shoulders I freeze.

For instance, the other night we were watching a video, and when he came up behind me and put his arms around me, I freaked out. I started to cry hysterically. I realize I still have triggers that remind me of Jakob. Sometimes my body reacts as if it is in trauma, and my mind doesn't even seem connected to my body. But my boyfriend is really understanding.

My Thoughts

Jasmine has worked hard to gain insight and forgive herself for the acquaintance abuse she suffered as a young girl. She has a supportive boyfriend, and over time, she has learned to trust him and enjoy their closeness. When Jasmine first came into our group, she was timid and frightened. As time went on, she became a lot more bold, and now she shares things more readily. It has been really inspirational for the other girls to see her in this healthy relationship with a guy. Her boyfriend drops her off at the group and picks her up, and they seem really happy. Jasmine has brought a couple of her friends to the group, too—other young women brought up in Israel who were molested as children. Jasmine has been a role model for many girls.

"I knew I needed to stop him, but I just froze with my

pride in my pocket."

Acquaintance abuse is a lot like date rape, in that the girl knows the person abusing her and chooses to be with him—but she doesn't choose to be sexual with him. Neither Jasmine nor Amber knew how to end the abuse. They were both preadolescent girls, and they were both vulnerable. Even though neither of them wanted the sexual attention, they both felt it made them special and were confused about whether they wanted to stop it. Amber felt special that a popular boy "wanted" her, and Jasmine felt pride that this "cool" boy paid attention to her.

I have found that girls who suffer acquaintance rape usually do not have an open dialogue in their families. They don't feel that their parents will or can help or guide them. This was certainly the case with both Amber and Jasmine's families. Jasmine's family might have been there for her, but her concern that she was going to be a bother kept her from going to them. This is also very common. It's hard enough for any girl to talk about sex and sexuality with her parents; especially when a girl is confused about whether she might have "asked for it," she can be too uncomfortable to discuss abuse with her parents.

As with all abuse, if you have suffered acquaintance abuse and are afraid to tell your parents, you can try calling a hotline or telling a trusted adult (a teacher or a friend, for example). You can also write about what happened in your journal. You might rehearse what you would say if you were to tell someone until you find the strength to say it. Even if the abuse happened years ago, writing about it and telling someone about it can make all the difference to how you feel inside. I can assure you that telling will help you feel better. Remember: Acquaintance abuse, even by a boy you like, is *never* your fault. You didn't deserve it. What you do deserve is the support to work through it. It's never too late to tell your story and begin to heal your wounds.

Chapter 10

Rape Always Hurts

Stranger Rape, Date Rape, Gang Rape

"I just don't let anyone get close. I protect myself by not allow-

ing anyone access to the control panels."

—AN EIGHTEEN-YEAR-OLD RAPE SURVIVOR

A lot has been written about rape over the past ten years or so. It's easy to forget that it was only twenty years ago that the first rape crisis center opened in New York City at St. Vincent's Hospital. Its founder, social worker Flora Colao, explains: "Rape was barely talked about then, but we kept getting women in the hospital who were being randomly raped, women so full of shame and fear that they were afraid to tell their husbands or anyone close to them."

We have come some distance since then. Many people, women and men, are working hard to change the laws and the courts. Women are writing books and songs and poems about rape and running rape crisis centers and hotlines, and we are grateful for all their efforts. But rape is still the number-one violent crime against women in the United States,[1] and we still have a long way to go. We must make people aware of the impact of rape on women; we must make the crime of rape seen and heard; and finally, we must prevent it.

One wonderful example of the ways young women are getting their voices heard comes from Brown University. In 1990, female students at Brown started scrawling the names of their accused rapists on the walls of the women's bathrooms. The attention this garnered drove Brown to require all first-year students to participate in a peer education program against sexual assault. Many other universities now also offer self-defense and rape awareness programs, some voluntary, some mandatory.[2]

Tori Amos sings an extraordinary, haunting song called "Me and a Gun" about her rape experience. It describes the time when she was nineteen years old and took a ride with a couple of guys who had been at her concert. They pulled over to the side of the road and raped her at gunpoint. In the song, which she sings a cappella, she talks about how the thought that she had never been to Barbados kept playing in her mind while she was being raped. Barbados became her metaphor for living through the ordeal.

So many young female rape survivors approached her after her concerts, she decided she had to do something about rape in America, and that is when she co-founded the Rape, Abuse, and Incest National Network, or RAINN, the largest rape crisis hotline in the country, perhaps in the world.

Through the past ten years, a number of women have also written books about their experiences of rape. In her book *After Silence: Rape and My Journey Back*, Nancy Venable Raine writes about a stranger rape that took place when she was thirty. Raine was taking out the garbage and left her apartment door open. When she returned to her apartment seconds later, a man raped her at knife-point. It took her ten years to write about it—ten years during which the rape continued to devastate her.

In *Where I Stopped: Remembering an Adolescent Rape*, Martha Ramsey looks back twenty years to detail her experience of being grabbed and raped in the woods when she was fourteen years old and riding her bicycle down a country road. She was still haunted by the rape twenty years later, she says, and needed to write about it.

Finally, as a society, we are "getting it" that women are still at risk, that rape is not rare but in fact rampant. Although all the books I just mentioned are about stranger rape, perhaps the most widely misunderstood rape crime—both by the general public and by victims themselves—is date rape. What makes date rape so confusing is that girls think they either should have or could have stopped it. And the fact is, it is one of the only forms of sexual abuse that can be prevented. That's why one of our goals in this chapter is to give you some tools to protect yourself from date rape. And it all starts with wising up and facing the dangers that can come with dating young men.

Rape Is An Epidemic

"I feel like my bulletproof vest has been shot through a thousand times, and I try to hold on, but it is all a bloody mess."

—A TWENTY-YEAR-OLD DATE-RAPE SURVIVOR

Girls and young women ages sixteen to twenty-five are at the greatest risk for date rape.[3] In fact, research into date rape on college campuses tells us that between 3 and 25 percent of college girls experience or are threatened with date rape.[4]

When you move away from home to begin college or for work, you are still testing the waters. You're figuring out who you are as an independent sexual being, and while you may want to revel in your new freedom and love the idea that you can party all night if you want to, you also have to be smart when it comes to sex and men.

Some girls are more vulnerable to date rape than others. Girls who were abused as children and never dealt with it are at far greater risk of being date-raped. When you are sexually abused and don't get help, the secret that someone sexually violated you still lives inside you and can eat away at you. You might still carry feelings of guilt or feel dirty inside. You might still be wondering, "Why me? I must have done something to bring the abuse on myself."

Depending on the kind of abuse you suffered, you might also feel as if you aren't good for anything else or that you somehow deserve to be treated badly. Many of these thoughts and feelings won't be conscious, but they will affect your behavior and your choices. That's why it's so important to talk about the abuse, write about it, get into a support group, or find a therapist. Even if the abuse happened years ago, you can get a lot of help and perspective by talking about it with trustworthy friends or adults.

Talking about it, you begin to root out that secret and all the ways it may be diminishing you, and you have a far better chance of dealing with whatever may come your way, be it warning signs of an abusive relationship, an attempted seduction by a mentor, or an attempted rape while on a date. When you start talking and get some help, you have a much better chance of being strong and of choosing healthy relationships.

Obviously, not all girls who were abused will be raped as older teenagers or young women, and not all girls who are date-raped were abused when they were younger. But there is definitely an important connection here, and we will be exploring the connection more fully in Iris and Dahlia's stories later in this chapter.

To all of you who are survivors of sexual abuse and are now attending college or moving into your own apartment for the first time, hear this: The abuse you suffered was not your fault. It's never the survivor's fault. Sexual abuse is rarely preventable; most of the time there is simply nothing a child can do about it. Children are at the mercy of adults, and very often, the path of least resistance is compliance. But that doesn't mean it was your fault. You have to believe that.

Many, many girls who survive sexual abuse but don't have anywhere to go with it turn to drugs and alcohol for comfort. They find ways to self-medicate—anything to avoid feeling the pain of what they've been through. That's often where their vulnerability lies—because drugs and alcohol impair our judgment. There are no two ways about it. If you're used to getting high or drunk to numb yourself from an earlier abuse experience, you are less likely to make the safest choices when it comes to going home with a guy. You may think that you have no voice, that sex is something you don't really have options about, that you have to take whatever the guy is dishing out. Sometimes you may not even be aware that you've been raped. If someone forces himself on you when you say no, you may feel that that's just the way it is. That's how out of whack unacknowledged, unhealed abuse can make you: You don't even realize that you are entitled to something much, much better.

If You've Never Been Abused, Are You Still at Risk?

We're hoping that girls who have never been abused are reading this, too. No matter how loving a family you may have come from, no matter how great and supportive your dad or brothers or uncles, you've got to understand that chivalry does not exist, especially when it comes to young men. You cannot expect boys to protect you; you can't count on them to respect your boundaries or to stop when you say stop. You need to be able to count on yourself.

In my work I've spoken with hundreds of boys, and I can tell you what they tell me: When a girl is drunk off her ass and fooling around, these boys feel they have the "right" to fuck them. That's the way they see it, girls—as their right.

I know this sounds harsh. I have had lots of people tell me it's not fair to paint all young men as potential predators. But I have to tell you the truth as I know it. Given the opportunity—the right time, the right place, and with drugs and/or alcohol present—most young men could force themselves on a girl, especially if they feel they are being led on and believe the girl "wants it."

Some enlightened young men do exist. We know that some young men volunteer to provide escort services to young women on college campuses. The trouble is, all boys see the same movies and read the same books as the rest of us. They are a part of the male culture that has its Humbert Humbert believing that Lolita "wanted it" when she was just twelve. They share the same locker-room mentality, where boys put another notch on their belt for every girl they fuck. That makes them the "mack daddy." This sexual violence against women will only change when men join the fight. According to Donald G. McPherson, the executive director of Sports Leadership Institute at Adelphi University in New York, an organization reaching out to male youth, "Boys and men must be involved in the fight against violence toward women because men are the perpetrators. As long as they perpetuate misogyny, there will be violence against women."

That's where the danger lies for girls. You may enjoy looking sexy, you may want to be sexual, and you may be turned on by a guy. But if you don't want to have intercourse with him, you can't count on him to respect you when you say no. You have to be prepared for this male-entitlement mentality that says, "She asked for it." Of course, you have the right not to have sex; you have the right to draw your own boundary lines. You may really enjoy kissing, touching, and holding, but if you don't want intercourse, don't go off drunk or stoned with a guy. Accurate statistics on rape are hard enough to come by and of course fluctuate from year to year, but the National Crime Victimization Survey conducted by the U.S. Department of Justice each year tells us that the vast majority of all reported rapes occur between people who know each other. You have to be smart about things and be prepared to protect yourself.

Unfortunately, an increasing number of women blame women for date rape—for not being savvy enough to stop it. For all the awareness that has developed around rape through the past ten years or more, there is a real backlash, too. Katie Roiphe, the daughter of renowned feminist Anne Roiphe, has written books and articles and has been all over the airwaves with her message that girls on college campuses must be asking for it if they are raped. She says it's your fault. In her book *The Morning After*, Roiphe casts doubt on the idea that young women mean no when they say no. She claims that no is sometimes part of the mating dance, and that you can't ask a boy to understand the difference between a no that means maybe and a no that really means no.

Then there's the old and disturbing saying, "If you can't stop the rape, you may as well lie back and enjoy it." This type of thinking only fuels people's woman-hating attitudes toward rape, and particularly date rape, and makes it that much harder to change public policy and the law.

Much misunderstanding about rape already exists. There's confusion about how it differs from sexual abuse. There's confusion about date rape versus stranger rape, and whether one is worse than the other. There's confusion about whether a girl has a right to say no to intercourse when she has otherwise been fooling around with a guy. There is confusion about whether you can be raped by your intimate partner. Some even say it's not really date rape if you meet a guy at a party and hook up, and then he forces you to have sex.

Let's be clear here: Anytime a woman resists having sex but is forced to do it anyway, that is rape or sexual abuse. Whether you say no, push the person away, cry, or try to run, if you are forced to have sex against your will, that is rape.

Many girls ask me if being forced into oral sex is rape. In my opinion, and in the opinion of other professionals, the answer is yes. While this might not hold up in a court of law because the legal definition may be more restrictive, any forced sexual entry is rape. That means if someone forces his penis into your mouth or forces anything into your vagina or anus, it is rape.

Let's get to some myths and truths.

MYTH: Rape and sexual abuse are the same thing.

TRUTH: While rape may occur as part of a longtime pattern of sexual abuse, rape can also be a one-time experience with a date, acquaintance, or stranger. Incest and other forms of long-term sexual abuse involve an ongoing relationship with the abuser and usually go on for some period of time. Sexual abuse usually involves coercion, false promises, or some kind of seduction.

While after a rape you may have some of the same feelings of violation, fear, and shame as you would after long periods of abuse, the two can cause different emotional scars. Sexual abuse by someone you know usually involves tangled issues of shame, guilt, and responsibility. Some of the aftereffects of stranger rape may be fear of the unknown, of the dark, of being alone, and a general mistrust of strangers, whereas incest causes a general mistrust of the people closest to you and of intimate relationships.

MYTH: You can't rape your own girlfriend or wife. That wouldn't be rape.

TRUTH: Rape does indeed happen between girlfriend and boyfriend, husband and wife. Men who force their girlfriends or wives into having sex are committing rape, period. The laws are blurry, and in some countries marital rape is legal, but it is still rape.[5]

MYTH: Alcohol and drugs may sometimes be involved in date rapes, but not usually.

TRUTH: According to Robin Warshaw in *I Never Called It Rape*, alcohol and/or drugs are known to be involved at least 75 percent of the time in date rape.[6]

MYTH: If a young woman comes on to a guy and wants to be sexual, she has no right to draw the line at intercourse and/or oral sex. If she's flirting heavily, she's "asking for it."

TRUTH: Just like young men, young women have the right to enjoy their sensuality and sexuality, including intense hooking up, and still say no to intercourse and/or oral sex. No one has the right to demand sex from another person under any circumstances.

MYTH: These days, most rapes get reported.

TRUTH: Very few rapes get reported.[7]

MYTH: Rape is against the law, so if you report a rape, there's a good chance that justice will be served.

TRUTH: The laws are still in flux, and most rapists are put back out on the streets, even after many arrests.[8] In October 2004, the Justice for All Act of 2004 was finally passed. This law provides approximately one billion dollars in funding over five years to eliminate the DNA backlog and improve the collection and processing of DNA in solving more rape cases. This law is known as the Debbie Smith Law, named for a woman who survived a stranger rape and fought for over fifteen years to get this law passed.

MYTH: Having an alcoholic blackout means you pass out, so you wouldn't even remember if you'd been raped.

TRUTH: It's true that you won't remember anything that happened to you during an alcoholic blackout, but you don't pass out. In fact, you are wide awake throughout. Alcoholic blackouts are periods of intoxication where you may seem awake and alert, but your brain is unable to form or store new information and experiences; in other words, you are out of it, even though your eyes may be open.

MYTH: Date-rape drugs are hard to come by.

TRUTH: Date-rape drugs are actually remarkably easy to get. They are used to incapacitate you and make you susceptible to sexual attack, and they can take away memory, not unlike an alcoholic blackout. With date-rape drugs, which are usually slipped into your drink and have no taste, you are passed out. You may wake up and have a strange sense that something happened or have no memory at all. There is also not just one date-rape drug. The familiar name heard on the streets and on college campuses is "roofies," short for Rohypnol, but you should also know that the following drugs can be used to induce a blackout for the purpose of date rape: Ativan, Xanax, and Benadryl—all commonly found on college campuses and easily obtainable.

MYTH: Stranger rape is more traumatic than date rape.

TRUTH: Generalizations like that are impossible to make. All rape is traumatic. Women who are raped will experience approximately the same symptoms, both physical and emotional, regardless of the type of rape. Stranger rape may make a woman fearful of walking alone or taking risks, but date rape is a major betrayal of trust. Who's to say which one is more damaging?

The Difference between Stranger Rape and Date Rape

Stranger rape is a terrifying violation that leaves many women frightened not only of strangers, but of all relationships. It can leave you feeling unprotected and unsupported by society, much as the incest survivor feels unprotected and unsupported by her family.

The biggest difference between stranger rape and other forms of sexual abuse is that being raped by a stranger doesn't usually cause the deep feelings of guilt and self-blame that come along with being raped by someone you agreed to be with. With stranger rape, it's much easier to understand that it wasn't your fault, but that does not eliminate the deep feelings of violation.

Another difference with stranger rape is that you usually fear for your life. More murders are reported in random stranger rape than in any form of sexual abuse between people who know each other, whether incest, acquaintance rape, or date rape. In her book *Lucky*, Alice Sebold describes seeing a pink hair tie in the leaves on the floor of the tunnel where she was brutally raped by a stranger at nineteen. She remembered that a girl had been raped and murdered in that same tunnel and felt "lucky" that she got out alive.

One of my clients had a similar experience. When she was raped at knife-point by a stranger who broke into her apartment, all she could think about was her baby daughter. She was twenty-eight at the time and had just returned home from a class. Her daughter was at daycare. The rapist, who had gagged her and tied her up before raping her at knife-point, told her repeatedly that he would kill her if she did not comply. She was more afraid of being killed than of the rape itself.

With incest, most girls know they will not be killed. They know the person raping them; they have a context. There is no context in stranger rape—just fear.

While the statistics on stranger rape are little better than those for any other kind of sexual abuse—as with other forms, most women don't want anyone to know—most professionals agree that stranger rape is reported more often than date or acquaintance rape, because the self-blame and confusion about responsibility involved in the latter are not factors.

What to Do If You Choose to Report a Rape

The first thing to do is *not* shower. It may feel absolutely awful to have to wait, but if you want the police to have evidence of the rape, you simply can't wash. Try to find a loved one or friend to come over and be with you and take you to the hospital. Once you get to the hospital, they will call the hospital's rape crisis unit. Things may vary by state, but usually you will be met by a rape crisis counselor/advocate who will walk you through the process of being examined and be there with you and for you throughout the examination. The hospital will then ask to collect what's called a "rape kit." Many girls get very nervous about the prospect of having to go through this procedure and don't know what their rights are. That's where the advocate can help you. Basically, no one can force you to get a rape kit; the hospital will not collect one without your consent. Remember that. The choice is yours. Also, getting the rape kit doesn't commit you to pressing charges; it only gathers evidence that might be extremely useful, and will sometimes be necessary, should you decide to prosecute.

If you do decide to get the rape kit, you should know what to expect. First of all, remember that you have the right to have your rape crisis advocate and/or loved one with you at all times. You also have the right to stop the process at any point.

What Is a Rape Kit?

1. You will be asked to disrobe, and a nurse will bag each article of your clothing—including, of course, your panties—to send to the crime lab.

2. Your pubic hair will be combed for any foreign hairs, and a sample of ten to fifteen of your own pubic hairs will be collected for comparison.

3. You will be examined for visible blood or semen stains. If such stains are found, samples will be collected.

4. You will be given a vaginal exam similar to a routine gynecological exam. Your vagina and cervix will be swabbed by a nurse.

5. Your fingernails will also be examined for blood, hair, or foreign tissue. If the nurse sees any foreign matter, she will also swab under your nails. A sample nail clipping may also be taken.

6. Your mouth will be swabbed for saliva.

7. If you report anal penetration, your anus may be swabbed as well.

8. The nurse will take a blood sample to check for infections and/or pregnancy.

9. And finally, a head-hair sample (ten to fifteen hairs) will be taken.[9]

Many times, for varying reasons, rapes are reported without a rape kit. Whether or not you get one, should you decide to report the rape or any other sexual abuse, here's what you can expect from the legal system (procedures vary from state to state, but this is more or less the sequence of events):

1. A detective will meet you to take down a report. You will be asked to describe what happened and to describe the suspect. (Remember, the decision to go ahead or stop is always yours.)

2. The detective will follow up with an investigation and may talk to witnesses and/or the person who assaulted you, if that person can be found. That person may or may not be arrested.

3. The detective will send a report to the District Attorney's office, and an attorney and advocate will be assigned to your case.

4. If an arrest is made, the defendant may be able to post bail.

5. The case will usually take a few years to prosecute.

Needless to say, this is a very quick sketch. If you want to know more about the complicated process of prosecuting sexual abuse and rape cases, check the Resource Center at the back of this book for further information.

Date Rape

When you are just walking down the street or riding your bike in the park or sleeping in your apartment and someone rapes you, there's no question that you didn't do anything to bring the rape on yourself. With date rape, it's entirely different; you do have more choices than you think. With date rape, you usually do have the power to prevent it.

Several of my clients suffered date rapes between the ages of eighteen and twenty. The two you will hear from were both nineteen when they were date-raped. Iris's date rape was her first and only experience of rape. Dahlia was date-raped after being violently gang-raped by acquaintances when she was fourteen. Both girls have emerged from these experiences to the other side and hope you will learn from their stories how important it is to take care of yourself. Understanding that you have the power to protect yourself from date rape by keeping your wits about you, having friends there to back you up, and not getting so stoned or drunk that your decision making is impaired can all protect you from date rape.

Iris

I met Iris when she was twenty-two and a senior in college. She had been raped three years earlier but had only recently come to terms with the fact that it was even a rape. In fact it was a male friend who convinced her that what she had experienced was date rape.

Since the rape, she had been in a string of bad relationships with men who did not appreciate her. She came to therapy because she had a sense that her rape of three years earlier had affected how she made choices in relationships. She also wanted to deal with her history of emotional abuse and connect the dots about why she kept picking such losers.

Iris had not been physically sexually abused as a child, but she had been emotionally abused and sexually abused verbally, and physically abused by her older brother. Iris comes from a Jewish family. She is the younger of two children; her brother is seven years her senior.

Both of their parents worked, and her brother was left in charge of her, beginning when she was seven and he was fourteen. That was when he started abusing her verbally. He would repeatedly taunt her. He would choke her, pinch her, make sexual comments about her breasts, her hips, and her rear end, and constantly tell her that she was a "worthless, ugly piece of shit." By constantly talking to her in sexual terms and touching her in inappropriate ways, her brother taught her that she had no right to any boundaries, physical or emotional.

As a child, Iris didn't know how to stop the sexual innuendoes or the inappropriate touching. Of course, in front of their parents, her brother behaved like an angel. Her parents trusted and praised their son, and when Iris complained about how he mistreated her, they ignored her.

When Iris began dating at around fifteen, she seemed to seek out males who would treat her badly. In hindsight, of course, that's no surprise. That's what she knew; that's what she felt she deserved. She put herself into many situations she should never have been in and struggled through adolescence with the feeling that she didn't deserve good relationships.

Fast-forward. Iris is now twenty-two and graduating at the top of her class from a prestigious university. She came in to see me because of her recurring nightmares, heightened anxiety, and depressive feelings. She had hit bottom and wanted to understand why she kept having dreams about the rape.

In Iris's story, she tells what it's like to be out partying with your friends, and what can happen as you get more and more drunk or high, how your judgment can blur, and how quickly your situation can escalate and get dangerous.

She talks about how she would get "buzzed" to deal with her insecurities and her very human need to fit in, and then describes the date rape and its aftermath in precise detail. She does not gloss over her rape in any way. I warn you: this is rough stuff. This is the unvarnished story of a date rape.

{ *Iris's Story* }

But I Thought He Liked Me

I was nineteen years old and had just finished my first year of college. A group of us were going out to celebrate the end of exams and the beginning of summer. We met at a club I had never been to. I loved the magic that took place when you entered a club. Through those guarded portals lay another world, a planet with an atmosphere all its own. Our group of three young women and two young men entered a room with swarms of people dancing to music, and I squinted as my eyes adjusted to the darkness. My head was fuzzy from the drinking I'd already done that night.

Our group met up with some other friends I did not know. There were people everywhere, drinking, talking, and popping pills. I was immediately attracted to a guy named Michael. He smiled a sweet, boyish smile when introduced to me, and I noted how handsome he was. He had large, dark eyes and a narrow goatee. I smiled back at him, more from self-consciousness than anything else. When I'd left the house that night, I'd thought I looked good, but when I looked at the people around me, they seemed to have stepped out of the pages of a fashion magazine. I felt like an impostor in the velvet-drenched, smoky scene. For more courage, I got another drink at the bar.

The bartender was a friend of a friend and had made us something special on the house. Sweet, fruity drinks usually made me sick, but I took a large gulp. It went down surprisingly smoothly, and I swallowed the rest of it quickly before my buzz had a chance to disappear. I wanted to drown myself in the stuff, let the pink liquid rise above my head as I danced. The alcohol pounded in my brain as if keeping time, my limbs gaining courage with every sip. Michael came over and danced with me. He was holding my back and swaying slowly from side to side, and my body responded. He was strong, and my lightness felt secure in his arms. The music got faster, and I started to move on my own in a sensual, drunken haze. He smiled down at me, grinding back. I was absorbed in the moment, in a capsule, all by myself. No external reality existed for me. All I knew at that moment was how good I felt, how good and free and light. We stopped dancing and got another drink and started talking, and I found him as charming and funny as he was handsome.

My friends then joined us. Ezra, a guy I had some classes with, came over and put his arm around me. He had been Michael's friend since high school, and after a while Ezra and Michael said, "Wanna get out of here?" I said good night to my girlfriend, who was also pretty drunk, and she winked at me, and we left.

My head was spinning wildly now, and I was starting to lose my balance. I should have listened to what my body was telling me: to have them drop me off at home so I could sleep the drunkenness off. I was drunk and tired, but I trusted Ezra, and I was attracted to Michael. I was dizzier than ever, slightly nauseous and stumbling, but I still thought I was all right. Michael and Ezra took me by the arms and held me up, and we stood there in front of the club, waiting for a taxi to take us home.

The next thing I knew, I was in bed in my apartment with no idea how I'd gotten there. My head felt like a swarming bee-hive, and as I opened my eyes, I saw Ezra crouched over me. He kissed me, the dry, alcoholic taste of his mouth mingling with mine, but I was dizzy. I wasn't aroused. I couldn't feel anything. Then, as quickly as he had begun, Ezra stopped kissing me. He pulled his face away from mine and looked down at me again. Michael came over. "I'm sorry," he said, starting to make his way down my body. "I just have to eat you."

I was so confused, the words meant nothing to me. I couldn't respond. Then Ezra appeared above me. I could feel my legs being pried apart and Michael sticking his face between them as Ezra shoved his tongue in my mouth. My body was numb, and I felt nothing, as if my nerve endings had been severed. As the drunken fog in my head began to clear, I realized what was happening. With the little strength I had, I got up and away from them and ran into the bathroom.

I was crying hysterically when Ezra came in. "What's the matter, baby?" he asked. I couldn't stop crying, couldn't talk; my body was shaking as I tried to speak. I tried to explain to him that I didn't know what was happening, that I was drunk and didn't want to do this. "Don't cry, baby, don't cry. I thought you liked Michael. You really want us to stop?" I nodded my head yes, suddenly exhausted, and he said okay, leaving me alone in the bathroom. The next thing I knew, I was lying on the bath-room floor alone, with closed eyes, having passed out again. My body was leaden, too heavy to move, and I wasn't sure where I was. The alcohol seemed thicker in my bloodstream now, moving slow as syrup, disorienting me. Before I could figure out where I was next, I felt my underwear being pulled off my body.

Realizing this was no dream, I opened my eyes and found Ezra gone. I had been dragged out of the bathroom and pulled to the floor in the bedroom, and Michael was kneeling in front of me. He was pulling my legs up around him and shoving his penis inside me. I was so tired, I was paralyzed. I felt like a rag doll, a limp creature with no skeletal structure or will of my own. It felt as if he was splitting me in half. I was torn between numbness and pain, and I asked him to stop. I opened my mouth to say no, but he rammed his tongue into my mouth hard. He kept pounding into me. I faded in and out, unable to stay awake. I kept trying to push him off me, I kept crying and struggling, and at one point I managed to get away.

I ran into the kitchen and hid behind the refrigerator. I was huddled back there shaking like a frightened animal. He followed me in and pulled me from behind it, lifting me like a feather and slamming me back down onto his penis. He propped me up against the countertop, driving me up and down on him like a butter churn, slamming my spine into the rough tile. Finally, he carried me back to bed to finish what he'd started. I realized I wasn't going to get away, and I almost willed my body to stay limp so I could disappear.

When he was done, he rolled over. I was allowed to fall back to sleep. I passed out from fear, exhaustion, and shock. When I woke up, the sun was up, and I heard noises in the apartment. I found myself on the floor. Michael was at the edge of the bed. He seemed large and awkward, mean spirited, uninterested. He was putting on his shoes.

"Hey, do you have a t-shirt I can borrow?" he asked.

I looked at him for a minute, confused, before lifting myself up from the floor. I rummaged through my dresser drawers for something that would fit him. "Thanks," he said, barely glancing up. Suddenly I felt ashamed. He continued dressing. I felt stupid and pathetic and frightened at the same time. He wasn't friendly; he wasn't nice at all. He grabbed his knapsack from the messy floor, littered with clothes—my clothes from the night before.

"See ya," he said, slamming the door behind him.

I stood for a moment watching the door, amazed that he could have disappeared so quickly. Tears were suddenly falling from my burning eyes. I smelled like smoke, and my mouth was dry and pasty, my vagina was bruised and burning and bleeding. There was dried blood all over my legs. The remnants of the alcohol nauseated me. My inner thighs ached, and my lower back stung. I saw bruises on my upper chest and my legs. I crawled back into bed, trying to figure out what had happened. All I wanted was for someone to tell me it would all be all right. I wanted to be held tenderly. I pulled the covers high over my head and lay like that for a long time, until I finally cried myself to sleep.

It took me a long time afterward to recognize what had happened to me. Unable to face the truth, I said to myself that I had been "rejected" by a guy I'd brought home who liked rough sex. That was a much easier pill to swallow than having been date-raped. I didn't talk about the experience to anyone. I basically put the incident in the back of my mind. I would run into Ezra from time to time, but he acted as if nothing had happened.

About one year after the incident I was describing it to a friend and he said, "Iris, you were raped!" I can honestly say that it hadn't hit me until then. I had been date-raped.

Three years after the incident, at twenty-two, I began therapy. I didn't know where to start. So I started to rehash the abuse I had experienced at the hands of my older brother. I began to understand that I had believed his lies; I had believed that no one would want me, so I was susceptible to any attention. In retrospect, I think I kept drinking that night because I was insecure and wanted Michael to like me. I came to therapy because I knew I needed to change. I was feeling insecure about graduating and finding a job, I was having nightmares, and my therapist explained that I needed to appreciate myself before I could commit to any relationship.

In the past two years, my therapy has been a journey to some places I didn't want to go. But I am finding that the more I talk about my childhood abuse at the hands of my brother and the lack of support from my parents, the more I am able to begin to stop blaming myself. As children, we have little to no control over the violations of our families—verbal, sexual, or physical—yet as young women, we can choose friends and lovers that do not treat us as our families did.

I have since learned that I do have boundaries. I have since learned that it is my responsibility, and no one else's, to make sure people respect me. As a child, I could not control my destiny. I could not get my parents to see the demoralization I had suffered at the hands of my brother. But as an adult, I get to choose to be around good people. I don't have to speak with my brother. I can limit my time with my parents if they are unsupportive. Slowly but surely, I am putting the rape behind me. I am learning that I am worth more. I have begun to heal.

My Thoughts

Iris wanted to share her story to help other young women avoid the mistake she made. She wants girls to know that they should not get drunk or stoned to the point where they make themselves vulnerable to danger. We also learn from her story that sometimes young women don't watch out for each other.

As she tells us, Iris did not have high self-esteem, and even though she was not physically molested as a child, the torment she suffered from the emotional and physical abuse by her brother convinced her that she deserved very little in relationships. No wonder Iris responded to the attention of these two males. After all those years of being told how ugly she was, just a crumb of positive attention felt great.

You'll recall that she knew, as she was getting drunk, that she didn't have all her faculties, but she trusted her "friend" Ezra. In fact, she drank so much that she passed out and went in and out of consciousness during the rape. She was so ashamed, she didn't even want to blame the rape on Ezra and Michael; it was easier to tell herself she'd been rejected by Michael.

I've seen many other girls who've blamed themselves for date rapes. They figure they're old enough that they should be able to keep things from getting out of hand. That's why date rape on college campuses is such a huge problem. Within the past ten years, date rape on college campuses has been identified as the number-one problem, with date and acquaintance rape topping the list of violent crimes against women on college campuses. And although in the past ten years we have made some progress by bringing this crime to the forefront, it remains a huge problem.

Many college girls are testing their new freedom; they do want to go out and get drunk and have a good time; they may even really be into the guy who takes them home. But that doesn't mean they asked to be raped. If a girl resists or says no or tries to run and a guy overpowers her, that is rape. All the backlash writing in the world doesn't change that fact.

Ask yourself a few questions: Is Iris's story so different from what could have happened to you on a night of parying? Do you and your friends watch each other's backs? Do you keep an eye on your drink at all times to be sure no one tampers with it? If there is ever a time where you can prevent being violated, date rape is it.

Acquaintance Rape, Gang Rape

"quick, call the cops

I've just been cocked blocked

Knocked out by a rock

My body was in shock

a flock of guys just left me alone

coughing up a bloody song

how could I whimper without a fight

I was weak and the cuffs were too tight "

—A TWENTY-YEAR-OLD GANG-RAPE SURVIVOR

In the story in Chapter 9 about Amber's experience of being manipulated into a molestation relationship with a counselor at summer camp, we noted the difference between acquaintance sexual abuse and incest. In this chapter, we've been talking about some of the differences between stranger rape and date rape. But there is also a difference between acquaintance rape and date rape.

Acquaintance rape usually refers to a situation where someone you know rapes you, but not on a date. Usually, you did not *choose* to be out or alone with this person. You may have ended up with him after being out in a group and never had any intention of being with him alone. Of course, at some basic level rape is rape, but getting raped after choosing to be with a guy feels a lot different from being raped by a guy you never had any interest in or attraction to in the first place. The former is more confusing, and you can really begin to question your judgment. It's upsetting in an entirely different way from when a stranger attacks you. Nevertheless, acquaintance rape can be just as traumatic.

Dahlia

When Dahlia was raped by some boys from school, she didn't even know any of their names. She'd only seen them in the halls at school. A girlfriend had brought her along to meet up with them in a park and then left her alone with these boys she didn't know.

Dahlia was only fourteen at the time. She grew up in San Francisco in its upscale Pacific Heights area. Her father was a very uptight guy, a successful banker and businessman. He made her feel worthless by his withering criticism. She was expected to get straight As and excel in sports. He also bullied her mother and younger brother. Dahlia never leaned on her mother for support; she just felt sorry for her. From a very young age, Dahlia learned to do everything she could to be perfect. She spoke softly and was always sweet and agreeable.

When she was eleven and her brother was eight, her parents got a messy divorce. Her father jerked her mother around about money, and her mother slipped into a quiet depression. Her brother became needy and demanding of both parents, and Dahlia, being the good girl, slipped into the background. She hardly ever saw her father and mostly just threw herself into her schoolwork and the track team.

Through Dahlia's riveting story, we learn how low self-image and constantly being in the background of her family can leave a girl vulnerable to rape and eating disorders. Again, a warning: This story is brutal.

{ *Dahlia's Story* }

I Was Scared They Would Kill Me

When I went to therapy at twenty, I felt like such an idiot. Not only was I raped once, I was raped twice! The first time I was clueless, but when I was nineteen I should have known better. Actually, I did know better. I knew I should have stopped drinking after the fifth drink. But I am insecure, and the drinking made me relax, so I kept going. A big mistake.

I am what some kids call a "mixed breed." Not a very nice way of saying I am half Chinese (my mom's Chinese) and half Irish Catholic (from my dad). I am kind of light-skinned for an Asian and have light brown hair. I call it mousy brown. I have always felt like kind of a freak, never really fitting in with either the Asian kids or the white kids.

My school was very rich and white. I always felt like I stood out. I guess you could say I still have a pretty bad self-image. People are always telling me how thin I am, but I don't agree. I think I'm much too fat. But I am trying to change those feelings. Track has always helped me to feel stronger and centered, but when I started to run to lose weight, it took some of the joy out of running. I am working on that, too.

I have always been a shy kid. When my parents separated when I was twelve, I was actually relieved. My father had the ability to scare the shit out of me just by entering the room. He never hit me or anything, but he was joyless, stern, and very judgmental. My mother is a sweetheart. I was really proud of her for breaking up with my father and going back to college at thirty-five. Asking for a divorce was the first time I ever saw her really stand up to my dad.

So there I was, twelve years old, a shy kid without a lot of friends. I spent most of my time alone, drawing in my sketchbook or writing in my journal. My seventh-grade year was mostly about helping my mom around the house and getting used to not having my father around to scare me, and my mom spent a lot of time calming my brother down. The year I entered eighth grade, I met another eighth grader on the track team, a girl named Lee Ann. Lee Ann was everything I wasn't. She was brazen, funny, and self-assured, and she even hung out with boys in the tenth and eleventh grades.

I wanted friends, I wanted to be invited along to things, so when Lee Ann asked me to go to the diner with her after track to get a sandwich, I said yes. Lee Ann then suggested that we go meet up with some guys she knew at Speedway Meadow in Golden Gate Park. Golden Gate Park is a huge park in the western part of San Francisco. It runs more than forty city blocks out toward the ocean and has lots of different areas: beautiful ponds, trails, fields, and lots of woods.

We all met up at the meadow at dusk. At first I was enjoying hanging out with these guys, even though I felt out of place. I had only seen them in the halls of school. They were all popular varsity football players and seemed pretty cool.

After a while, Lee Ann announced that she had to go. When I tried to leave with her, one of the boys knocked me down. Weird. I thought it was an accident, but then Lee Ann turned to look and saw me on the ground and just left me there. That's when I got scared.

As I got up, another boy grabbed me by the arm. I tried to yank myself free. I told them I was leaving, but one of the boys took off his sock and stuffed it in my mouth. I couldn't make a sound. I think I was in shock.

The three boys dragged me into a secluded woody area. It was dark by then. One boy pushed me down, another pulled down my pants, and the third unzipped his pants and forced his penis into me. I remember the boys laughing. Then one boy started jerking off, his sperm hitting me on my head, while the third boy took his turn with me. Even though this all probably lasted about fifteen minutes, it felt like hours.

When they were all done, they threatened to kill me if I told. They said they'd hurt my little brother and my mother. They recited my address and phone number and told me they'd be watching me "all the time." Then they left me with the sock stuffed in my mouth, my pants and underpants all ripped and bloody, and gunk all over my hair and face.

I am not sure how I got myself up and got home, but I did. I was so relieved that no one was home when I got there. I headed straight for the shower, still feeling numb. In the shower, I finally started realizing what had happened. I began to sob and just sat at the bottom of the shower, holding myself and rocking back and forth.

When my mother and brother came home a little while later, my mom called up the stairs. I quickly threw on some clothes and came down to join them as if nothing had happened. My mom asked about the bruise on my forehead, but I just told her that I had fallen during track and not to worry. My mom, having no reason to suspect anything, believed me.

I couldn't sleep that night. I felt as if I was crawling out of my skin. I looked at my bruises and remembered them pushing and pushing until my skin was scraped bare. They'd taken all my hope and ripped it out of me. When my mom came up that night to kiss me goodnight, I almost jumped out of my skin in fear. I told her I felt sick.

That night I woke up in a cold sweat. I had come down with a fever, and my mom agreed that I should stay home for a couple of days. I was terrified to go to school; I was terrified the boys would find me in the halls and torment me. I believed they would come after me again, and I was terrified that they would come after my family if I told. After the brutality of the gang rape, and their laughter, I figured they were capable of anything, even killing. What did I know? I was just a young kid.

Even though I was scared to go back to school, I wanted to see Lee Ann and say to her, "Fuck you for leaving me alone with those assholes in the park." I didn't know if she knew or had even maybe set me up. I mean, the way she'd turned and looked and then ridden off on her bike . . . I thought, she must have known they were going to do something to me. I lay there in bed thinking about their sick smiles and laughter, the spitting, the jerking off, and I just cried and cried.

Meanwhile, my mother was crying herself to sleep every night. It's a really shameful thing in the Asian culture to get divorced, and my mother's family had shunned her and actually taken my father's side. I certainly wasn't going to burden my mom with my problems. I believed I was her lifeline.

On Friday I finally went to school. I saw Lee Ann in the halls, and she said hi really nonchalantly. I couldn't believe it. I was practically shaking the whole time, but I did draw up the courage to ask her why she had left me alone with those assholes in the park. She said, "Oh, they said they had a great time with you!" That froze me. I just avoided Lee Ann from then on. I didn't know whom I could trust.

I spent months being petrified that these guys would do something to me or to my family if I told. I retreated into my own little hell. I never spoke to Lee Ann, but I avoided everyone, really. I always looked over my shoulder for those asshole boys, and I tried to always leave my classes with classmates and to never walk alone in the halls.

The boys did see me a couple of times. Once they even followed me home, jeering and whispering, "Better not tell, bitch." One time, they cornered me at my locker when the halls were deserted. They pushed me up against the locker and threatened me again, saying they were watching me and my little brother, and that I should watch my back. After school ended for the year, they seemed to leave me alone. Who knows? Maybe they'd raped another girl by then. But I was still frightened all the time.

I felt out of control. Now running track was not enough. I needed to control something else, and about the only other thing I could control was my eating. So I started to count every calorie of everything I put into my mouth, and then I would vomit after almost every meal. I bought cookbooks and read the calorie content of all foods; I figured out ways to pretend I had eaten what was on my plate by putting food in napkins at the dinner table. And I think this little bit of control saved me from going totally crazy.

Meanwhile, my mother was pretty clueless. My father was always away on business so I barely saw him, and my brother was having a lot of trouble in school, so nobody was really paying attention to me. I used to cover up my body with double layers of t-shirts and everything, so I guess nobody really knew how thin I had become. No one knew, either, that I would vomit after every meal. I know it sounds awful, but the vomiting felt like getting rid of all the bad stuff that had been building up inside me.

I was scared and tormented by the rape, but I never told anyone what had happened to me. I continued to do well in school, avoided most kids, and finished eighth grade.

The next fall, I started ninth grade, and about thirty new kids entered our public school from the next town over. I made the varsity track team and actually started to become friends with a couple of new girls at school. I would still see the boys who raped me in the halls at school from time to time—they were seniors now, and they thought they ruled the school—but they had stopped paying any attention to me. I was still scared to death inside, but I found great comfort in being obsessed with food and weight and calories.

Ninth grade was when my body started to betray me. Even though my period had started when I was twelve, it had stopped with my eating problem. But now my breasts had started growing, and boys were checking me out. This made me totally anxious. Whenever a guy would look at me or try to hang out with me, I would panic. I tried never to walk the halls alone. I always tried to be with one of the new kids. My reputation at school was that I was some guy-hating weirdo. Some kids even started rumors that I was gay. That didn't bother me so much, but the stares from guys did, so I ate even less. Still, nobody noticed. My mother was busy with college, and most of my friends were almost as obsessed with calories as I was.

My little world at the time revolved around eating and purging, around counting calories and checking for pinchable flesh. I was determined never to have any flesh that could be pinched. I figured that if I didn't look like a woman, if I had no curves, no breasts, no flesh, maybe I wouldn't be rape-able, maybe I wouldn't be sexual. Maybe I would disappear.

Finally my mother became concerned. She finally noticed that I had become reclusive and frail and less and less communicative. She tried to talk to me, tried to get me to eat. But I would get defensive, and my mom and I started fighting a lot. She was doing better, and I was pissed. I was pissed if she tried to tell me what to eat and what not to eat. I hated her commenting on my body and felt invaded when she said anything about my looks.

Then one day at track practice, I passed out on the field and had to be taken to the emergency room of our local hospital. I weighed just eighty-seven pounds. I was immediately given an IV and came in and out of consciousness. I think they were sedating me, and the IV was making me nauseous. After two days they transferred me, or, I should say, my mother committed me, to a psychiatric hospital. I hated that place. I had to go to group therapy with boys; kids were hooking up on the unit while the staff wasn't looking; and girls were vomiting and taking enemas to keep their weight down and then drinking gallons of water and not peeing for weigh-in. Wow, I was learning all kinds of tricks in the hospital.

I really wanted to get out. The social worker kept asking me over and over why I was so depressed, why I was anorexic and bulimic, why, why, why. I hated her. Finally one day in a family therapy session I blurted it all out about the rape. It was me and my mother and the social worker. My mother leapt from her chair and grabbed hold of me. It felt really good to finally let out the secret, but I made them promise it wouldn't go past that room.

Three weeks after that meeting, I left the psych hospital. I had my new survival techniques (enemas, water retention) and felt a mixture of relief and terror that I had told. Even though I'd asked her not to, my mother told my father, and they insisted that I press charges. I told them that was impossible. I was too scared. I told them that the boys weren't reachable anymore, that they'd graduated and gone to college and moved out of town. But my parents insisted.

Before the boys were notified or any charges pressed, I was grilled by the attorney, and everything got dredged up again, and I went into a major depression. My anorexia was in high gear because I felt all over again that all my power was being taken away from me.

When we showed up for another appointment with the lawyer, I fainted and needed another hospitalization. This time, I was put into a regular hospital, and my weight was "normal" at ninety-two pounds, so I was released with a sedative. I begged my parents to drop the case. They agreed.

After the case was dropped, I made a deal with myself that I would keep myself so busy I wouldn't have time to think or remember anything. I refused therapy. I became obsessed with track, school, and, of course, calories. Now I knew the price of going under the required ninety-two pounds. It was tricky, but I managed to maintain that "healthy" weight. I somehow finished high school with honors and got accepted into an Ivy League college with a track scholarship. I had put the gang rape way down deep into a dark place that I never went to.

My first year at college went smoothly, and then the summer after my freshman year, I got raped again. This time it was a date rape. The next thing I knew, I was sitting in Dr. Patti's office, with my roommate who brought me there.

My Thoughts

The summer after her freshman year, Dahlia had been out on a date with a guy she'd just met. She was nervous and had drunk herself into oblivion. They started fooling around a little, but when he wanted to keep going, she said no. This time she screamed. It didn't matter. He raped her anyway. Dahlia waited a couple of days to tell; then she told her roommate, who was also an abuse survivor. Her roommate was one of my clients and brought her in to see me. We immediately began to peel away the layers of Dahlia's traumas.

It has been two years since that first session, and Dahlia still struggles with her weight. She is afraid of relationships with males, but at least now she has a good female friend, her roommate. Dahlia is still haunted that she never went through with the case against the sick boys who gang-raped her, but the truth is she is, still not strong enough to do so. Not all girls have the strength to report their rapists or molesters. And that has to be all right, too.

Of course we all want to see justice done, but sometimes justice is served when a girl can sleep through the night without a nightmare. Although Dahlia still struggles with her eating disorder and still gets depressed, she has not been out drunk with a guy since her date rape. And in our last session, she talked about accepting a date with a really nice guy she had met at school. That's justice, too.

Where Will It End?

Rape is an epidemic, and while the laws have gotten better over the years, they do not protect women from rape. Police follow-up on rape is terrible. According to Kellie Greene, the director of Speaking Out About Rape (SOAR), 169,000 rape kits are just sitting in police departments across the country, not being tested. Most rapists are never caught, and if they are, they're rarely prosecuted, and if they're prosecuted, they almost never go to jail, and if they go to jail, they're usually back on the street at the speed of light.

At this point, we cannot count on the police or the courts to protect us from rape. And our culture doesn't help. There is more pornography available now than ever before, not to mention the general "pornographication" of young women. It's no surprise that the director of many Britney Spears videos is Gregory Dark, a well-known hardcore pornographic-movie director. The Britney Spearses and Christina Aguileras of the world are everpresent, making it even more difficult for young women to actually enjoy being sexy without the shadow of explicit sexual provocation hanging over them.

Young women have the right to love their bodies, to enjoy their sexuality, to connect love and sex. And many young women do. But there's never been a greater need to be smart about it. Boys are susceptible to those sexualized images of young girls and are demanding sex at younger and younger ages.

All that said, there are ways to be smart and to take steps to stay as safe as you can. The following tips will help you remain aware of potentially risky situations. Remember these pointers and pass them on to your friends.

Pointers Against Date Rape

1. Keep your wits about you when you are out. Do not get stoned or drunk to the point of oblivion.

2. When you do go out with friends, make sure they have your back. Always have one friend aware that you are partying, and take turns being on call for each other.

3. If you are out partying and the guy you are with is also drunk or stoned, do not go off alone with him unless you are ready to defend yourself from a rape. That may sound alarmist, but let's face it, girls, this is our culture. Of course, not all boys or men are rapists in waiting, but why play with fire when there are ways to protect yourself?

4. Understand that alcohol and drugs impair your judgment.

5. Never leave your drink unattended so that someone could put a pill in it.

6. Never go off alone with a guy you don't know. It's just not safe. If you meet a guy and like him, your best bet is to go out with him several times in a group before going anywhere with him alone.

7. Make your intentions clear. If you are not interested in sex, let the guy you are with know that. Remember, you are entitled to set the boundaries on physical contact.

Some girls who have been date-raped even report that when they snapped to and became aware that they were being forced into sex, they had enough physical strength to push the guy off and get away. As far as stranger rape goes, there is not that much you can do to protect yourself because of the randomness of the crime, but turn the page to find some additional words to the wise.

1. Needless to say, you are far less likely to get raped in the afternoon on a busy street than at 2:00 AM walking alone on a deserted street.

2. Large parking lots are notorious for rapes, so always try to park in a crowded, well-lit, preferably outdoor lot.

3. Walk tall and proud.

4. Don't be dialing up on your cell phone or oblivious to your surroundings, deep in conversation.

5. Don't look vulnerable. This cannot always prevent a random rape, but it may help.

6. Take a self-defense class. This will make you feel more in control of your body.

All that said, during stranger rape, when someone has a knife to your throat, all the strength or self-defense skills in the world might not help you. But it can be very empowering to know that you have some skills to fight back if a guy is trying to force sex on you.

Most important, be there for your friends. If your friend is raped, be there for her, but also be there to help each other to have a good time when you are out partying. Always have a designated girl to stay sober and be on the watch. Help each other, girls. Support each other and enlist the good guys to stand tall with you.

PART FOUR
THE ROAD BACK

Chapter 11

Different Paths to Healing

*"All the men that have crossed my path have hurt me, invading
the journey I was supposed to be on. I have been tampered with
and washed up. I am clearing out a new path now."*

—A TWENTY-YEAR-OLD INCEST AND RAPE SURVIVOR

As we've seen, there are many different paths to healing. You've heard
from many girls by now, and although their experiences varied, each of
them spoke about how they were able to move on in their lives once they
spoke out about their abuse. This was their primary means to healing.

Throughout the book, we have seen how powerful telling your story can
be, and as you move through the various feelings that result, you might want
to take some further action. Much of this book is about dealing with your
sexual abuse once you have already left your home, because that's when
most girls have their first real opportunity to get some perspective and to
heal. As much as I understand how difficult and perhaps impossible it can
be to leave home before you are eighteen, one important purpose of this book
is to open new pathways for you. If you are still living at home, make a list
of all the adults you know and figure out who might take you in, who
would support you, and who would help you get away from your abuser. Use
your sixth sense. You'll know if you have the option to leave.

Trying to move out before you're eighteen might involve you in a
court case, but if you feel you have a good option for getting away from your
abuser, you might choose to go ahead anyway.

Beyond telling and getting away, however, there are an awful lot of
myths out there about how to move on or get "justice." People may tell you

to report the crime or confront your abuser—or even to forgive him. I don't necessarily advocate any of these things. I think counseling of some kind can be enormously useful, but the bottom line is that the main way to heal is to find people who will support you, to talk about what happened, and to ground yourself in the reality that the abuse was not your fault, that you have nothing to be ashamed of, and that you deserve great love and happiness in your life. But I would be remiss were I not to at least look at some of the paths that some girls take and to give you some information.

Should You Report the Crime?

Throughout this book, we've been talking about how important it is to tell someone what happened to you, to choose wisely whom you tell, and to get support. You should know that no matter what kind of sexual abuse you've endured, you may be encouraged to report what happened to the police. That's not necessarily the kind of telling that is important for your healing. Many girls who have been sexually abused don't want to get the police involved. They don't want to press charges and have to face the legal system. And that's completely understandable.

Some instances of sexual abuse, especially if they happened in the distant past, would be too hard to prove. When the abuser is a family member, girls are often pressured by their families not to press charges and cause the family embarrassment. Girls also know that they'd need iron wills to be able to withstand all the interviews, getting up on the witness stand, telling their stories publicly, and often brutal cross-examinations that dredge up every intimate detail of a girl's life, to make no mention of low prosecution rates. Every girl has to ask herself if it's worth reporting the crime in her particular case. For many, the answer will be no, and that is okay.

Many girls who choose to report end up feeling violated all over again by the criminal justice system. The process can really stink. The one good reason I can think of to report your abuse and press charges is when your abuser is likely to be a danger to other girls. As we will see in Pearl's story in Chapter 12, for example, Pearl stepped forward and told when she became afraid that her uncle was abusing her younger sister. She told with the hope that by telling she would stop him.

Pearl told her guidance counselor about her uncle, and her counselor called the police, as he was required to do. Police came to the school and spoke with Pearl. They also interviewed me, because she had disclosed the abuse to me and given me extensive details. They took my verbal and written word as evidence, and I was considered a witness to the disclosure.

With the support of her family, Pearl pressed charges against her uncle. An order of protection was issued that prohibited him from having any contact with Pearl. Her uncle then pleaded guilty to the charges, and the case was settled out of court. This was a positive thing for Pearl. Going to court can be a very difficult part of the process for a girl—having to face your abuser, tell your story over and over again in detail, and have all the intimate details of your life become public property.

In Pearl's uncle's case, because the abuse had taken place seven years prior to the disclosure, he received only a very light sentence: probation and mandatory counseling for a year. It seems that he never went after Pearl's sister again, but now some allegations of sexual abuse have been made against him by other girls. Was it worth it for Pearl to report the abuse and press charges against her uncle? Maybe. It did prove to her that her parents were squarely in her corner, and that in itself helped her heal from the abuse. But then there was Garnet, who also reported the abuse; nothing was done because her father managed to convince the police that he was innocent, and her sister refused to corroborate the abuse—and then ended up living on the streets as a prostitute.

I have a client who did report an acquaintance rape to the police. They pressured her to wear a wire and meet with the rapist, and at that meeting, he once again attempted to rape her. The police intervened, but even with a witness and good solid proof, this rapist was jailed for only six months.

And then there is Emily, whom you'll read about in Chapter 12 and who, during a custody trial in family court, did report her father's abuse; the judge allowed his visitation rights to continue—albeit under supervision—until further information could be gathered.

Many counselors and police detectives will tell you that it's always best to report the crime. That may serve them and give them useful data. And it may be right for you. But you must never let anyone force you to report abuse. And the people around you should support your choice. If they don't, remind them that it is your choice. If you think there's little chance that you can prove that the abuse took place (if it was years ago, or if there were no witnesses and you didn't undergo a medical exam), you have to ask yourself what is to be gained by reporting. Only you can make the right choice for you. I feel the same way about confronting your abuser. If you don't want to, don't. This is about your healing and no one else's.

All that said, the criminal justice system is far more responsive and respectful of women now than it was, say, thirty years ago. If you decide that prosecuting is part of speaking your truth and healing, then use the criminal justice system well. Be prepared, have advocates, and know that no matter what happens in the courts, you have spoken your truth, and it was not your fault. The legal route is certainly not for everyone. Only you can decide if it's right for you. The Resource Center at the back of this book has more information.

Should You Confront Your Abuser?

"You fat fuck of a blood-sucking villain. The time has come for me

to squash my mosquitoes, and you, buddy, are the first to go."

—A SEVENTEEN-YEAR-OLD RAPE SURVIVOR

This quote is from a poem in a rape survivor's journal. She never confronted the rapist, but she sure is confrontational in her writing, and that has been a huge factor in her healing. There are many types of confrontation. The most important thing is that you confront, in your own mind, the truth that your abuser is the guilty party.

Many girls ask if they should confront their abuser directly. My short answer is no.

That said, if you somehow end up in the court system, either by choice or because your parents insist on it, you will be forced to see your abuser in court, to look at him and speak about what happened. You may have been told or read somewhere that confronting your abuser, in person, in a letter, in a phone call, will help you heal. That has not been my experience at all. Confronting your abuser could have almost nothing to do with healing. I have seen many cases where girls were pushed to confront their abusers and it only hurt them more. I think it's simply a fallacy that by telling the abuser what he did to you and airing your feelings, you will somehow feel better. Much of the time, your abuser will just deny everything anyway.

You remember Garnet, whose father completely dismissed her when she confronted him? He told her no one would believe her. That's when she started to feel totally despondent and turned to drugs, drinking, and self-harm. She had hoped that confronting him would bring her relief, and all she got was violated all over again.

If you feel the need to say something to your abuser directly, you could try writing a letter and burning it. You could write songs and poetry. But don't ever expect your abuser to make you feel better, because he never will. Even if you confront him and he cries and apologizes, things don't necessarily get better. You may even begin to feel sorry for him, which will only lead to greater confusion. Whatever you do, just remember: This is about *you*, not *him*. His response isn't important; only choose to confront him if it will make *you* feel better.

I'll say it again. You do not need to confront your abuser, and I don't recommend it. Most of the time, your best bet is to get away and work through your process away from him. I have worked with hundreds of girls who have healed without ever directly confronting their abusers.

Should You Forgive Your Abuser?

"I wanted so many times to simply have faith, to give my soul over to the care of something else, someone else, because there were times when it just felt too filthy for me to hold anymore. But then there was always some rule, like 'turn the other cheek' or 'forgive and forget.' Some concept of forgiveness that I couldn't even wrap my brain around. It seemed so incomprehensible. How do you 'forgive' someone for taking away your childhood, your wonder and your innocence and your 'first time' and your chance to discover yourself without dark pits and chasms open-

ing up underneath you on the path? Maybe some people can
forgive, but I always knew in my gut that I wouldn't. It felt like a
copout, like maybe if I avoided feeling angry about this, then my
world would stay the way it was on the surface, ordinary and
cheerleader-y. I am angry, and I know I don't have to 'walk a mile
in my stepfather's shoes.' I don't give a damn about his pain or
'why' he did what he did to me."

—A TWENTY-TWO-YEAR-OLD INCEST SURVIVOR

I cannot tell you how many young women survivors come to me having been told by a well-intentioned therapist, clergyperson, or even their own mothers to forgive their abuser. I say no. No, no, and no. The only person you need to forgive for your healing is *yourself*. I have seen too many girls who tried to forgive ending up right back where they started, believing they were at fault in the abuse. As far as I'm concerned, forgiveness is just a kind of gift to your abuser. He is 100 percent responsible for what happened to you. You don't owe him a thing.

Of course you need to make peace with your own faith, and if your faith tells you you need to forgive in order to come through, I would never want to stop you from doing that. Although there are different schools of thought, I believe clinically and psychologically that forgiveness is not necessary for healing.

It's almost always best to make a clean break, surround yourself with supportive people, express your emotions to people you can trust, and not worry about confrontation or forgiveness or getting closure in that way. With good support, you can get over this. It's not something your abuser can do for you. You don't have to allow him any more space in your heart or any more access to your body or soul.

Your mother may have forgiven your father or stepfather for molesting you. Your abuser may have served his (usually pitifully brief) time and then come back home to live with you. Maybe your parents dragged you to family therapy and forced you to learn to "forgive." I think this is almost criminal. I have seen this wound girls deeply and spill over into how they feel about themselves for years. If you find yourself in this scenario, please try to find people to support you. When you have the opportunity to move out, you will have the choice not to be part of a family that forgives the father who raped you.

Should You Go for Therapy?

"When my therapist told me the incest was not my fault and that my father was evil, I just sat there and cried."

—AN EIGHTEEN-YEAR-OLD INCEST SURVIVOR

At many points along this journey, you may find yourself wanting to talk to a professional. Fortunately, there's more and more help out there. There are hotlines, crisis counselors, social workers, and therapists, just for starters. In fact, in most states now there are rape crisis centers where you will receive free counseling.

You might want to start with a hotline. The fact that the person on the other end of the phone doesn't know you can make it a lot less scary to open up. I have known girls who have called hotlines many times, even twenty times, before they were ready to tell someone they knew. The women answering the phones are often survivors themselves and lend a very understanding ear. They won't advise you unless you ask for specific advice; they'll just listen to you and support you.

If you're ready for face-to-face counseling, just be sure that the counselor is someone you trust completely. Of course, it doesn't have to be a professional. Just find someone who cares about you.

Please understand that if you are under eighteen and abuse is still taking place in your home, any teacher or counselor you tell at your school is obligated to report the abuse. Of course, if you know the counselor or if s/he is very experienced and sensitive, s/he *will* help you with the report, but s/he will be obligated, legally, to make a report. If you are no longer in danger, s/he won't have that legal obligation, and you may feel freer to open up.

Even though I am a therapist, I want to tell you that therapy is not the only way to heal. If you open up and find support and love, you will find healing. There are also some pretty amazing novels and films listed in our

Resource Center that may really resonate with you and be part of your path to healing. You will also find a couple of healing workbooks in the Resource Center that may help you. And remember, running, singing, talking, playing, drawing, painting, dancing, and any other way you express yourself helps you heal. Let it go, get it out, and you will move on.

But if you do choose some form of therapy, the most important thing is to feel comfortable with your therapist. No matter how much training or how many degrees your therapist has, if you don't like her or him, the therapy probably won't help you.

Sometimes the experience of being in counseling with a therapist you can't relate to can make you feel even more isolated. If you feel that your therapist has too much power or control over you, you may re-experience the abuse feelings. If that's the case, don't stick around. Even if your parents are forcing therapy on you, they can't pick the person you are going to feel the most comfortable with. Only you can do that. So keep interviewing until you find the right person.

Helpful Hints for Finding a Therapist

1. Make sure you "click" with the therapist and feel unconditionally supported. (If the therapist tells you to leave this stuff in the past and not talk about it, run—don't walk—out of her office.)

2. Keep looking until you find someone you can afford. Many clinics offer free or low-cost counseling to sexual-abuse survivors.

3. Find a female therapist if you possibly can. You might not feel all that comfortable talking about sex with a man, but this is a decision you have to make.

4. Never allow yourself to be forced to talk about anything you're not ready for.

5. If you are under eighteen and currently surviving incest, your

therapist will be legally bound to report the crime, but a good therapist will consult you and work it out with you before she does anything.

6. Be aware that everything said in your sessions should be kept confidential, even from your parents, unless you are a harm to yourself or others.

7. Take your time. Find the right counselor. Get well. Allow yourself the time to heal.

One of my sixteen-year-old clients defines therapy beautifully. She says that she goes in and dumps all her problems on the floor, as if scattering papers. We pick one up, we look at it, we put it down. We pick up another, we work it through, we rip it up, we throw it away. And at the end of the session, we gather up all these papers and put them in a special box, up on a shelf, and leave it in my office until the next session.

One of the great benefits of therapy is that in many ways it is a one-way relationship. You do not have to worry about the therapist. She is there to help you, never to burden you with any of her personal problems. She is there *for you*.

※　　※　　※

Healing does not necessarily come from reporting or confronting your abuser, and it certainly does not come from forgiving him. Don't let anyone pressure you into doing any of these things. Healing comes from speaking about your experience, letting out your secrets. It is a process of forgiving yourself. Healing comes from loving yourself and trusting yourself. Healing comes when you realize that your abuser is to blame, when you are able to slough off the feelings of shame and guilt. This is a very different process for every girl and every young woman. This is your life, and you deserve to walk your own path in healing.

Chapter 12

Supportive Families Speak Out

"When my husband found out that his brother had molested our
daughter, he went to his home, pushed him to the floor, and
started to bash his head in."

—A MOTHER OF AN INCEST SURVIVOR

So far, we have heard a lot about families who sit by and do nothing to protect their daughters from abuse. We have heard about parents who loved their daughters but were blind to what was going on, mothers who had never dealt with their own childhood sexual abuse, and who married men who then molested their daughters, mothers who stood by their husbands even after the abuse was reported, fathers who were so evil that they raped their daughters and told them it was their right to do so.

Needless to say, most people do not want girls to be raped, molested, and harmed, and most parents don't let such things happen; they would never tolerate anyone hurting their child. Most of us feel rage toward molesters, rapists, and abusers.

The following stories bring us into the worlds of some of these betrayed families. As you'll see, many girls do have allies within their families. And you may be surprised to learn that often it takes parents much longer to heal than it does daughters. Girls are incredibly resilient, but long after their own scars from abuse have healed, their parents are often still dealing with theirs. Nonetheless, the single most important thing the parent of a sexually abused girl can do is show unconditional support.

Jannie's father literally had a heart attack after hearing about her abuse and trying to confront the abuser. Her mother still believes his heart gave out because he could not bear his daughter's abuse or the injustice that followed.

{ *Jannie's Mother's Story* }

A Mother's Loss

"They were mean to me. They made me do things I didn't want to do." These words will haunt me for the rest of my life.

When my daughter Jannie was nine years old, she went to spend a weekend at her friend Amy's summer home in a chic area of the Jersey Shore, a hundred miles away from our Upper West Side Manhattan home. Jannie had really been looking forward to this weekend away, the last summer weekend before school. We knew Amy's parents and certainly trusted them with the care of our only child, but I hadn't wanted her to go. Before she left, I explained that we could not pick her up if she wasn't having a good time and said that we'd see her in three days. She seemed to understand.

When Jannie got home three days later, she went straight to her room and curled up on her bed. She made me come with her and begged me to stay with her until she fell asleep. Just before she dozed off she uttered these haunting words: "They were so mean to me. They made me do things I didn't want to do." I asked her what they made her do, but she wouldn't answer. She made me check under the bed for "men" and assure her that no one could enter her window (on the twelfth floor!). This was very atypical behavior for Jannie, and I again asked her what had happened, but again she did not answer. I thought perhaps they'd made her eat peas and carrots or something trivial like that. I remember being a bit annoyed and acting abrupt.

Jannie woke up the next morning and went off to school just fine. She seemed all right. And for eight years, she never mentioned that weekend again. I will never forgive myself for being so flip and maybe making her feel that she couldn't talk to me. I can't stop thinking about how I didn't press the issue or beg her to tell me what she meant by those ominous words. It taught me that you should never trivialize what a child says to you.

Jannie's adolescent years were very rocky. She had learning problems and hence some of the other problems that typically result—feeling a bit left out socially, bouts with depression. We were a loving family, but I guess our love wasn't enough to take away Jannie's depression.

At age sixteen, Jannie made a suicide attempt and was hospitalized. It was in a family therapy session in the hospital that we learned what had happened to Jannie on that weekend so many years before.

Amy's father had brutally raped and sodomized Jannie. She had just turned nine years old. He told her that if she was a good girl and never ever told anyone, he would not do it again. He told her that it was a very private, important secret, and that harm would come to her family if she told. He pricked his finger with a pin and then pricked hers, and then put their fingers together and explained that this gave them a blood connection. He exploited my poor little girl's insecurity over being adopted. How sick is that? He also said that because she was adopted, she could be taken away from us if she told.

Well, she believed this man, this so-called pillar of the church and community. And she never told until she had to because she was crawling out of her skin.

When my husband heard Jannie describe the rape, he totally lost it. He made us go to their house straight from the hospital, and he practically broke his hand banging on the door. They let us in, of course, and my husband lunged at the father. His wife and I had to pull him off. At that point, we noticed their daughter Amy crawl under the table. My husband was so enraged he had a heart attack.

After his hospitalization, we began legal proceedings. As helpful and nice as all the police and lawyers were, they made it clear that our daughter would have to testify. Initially, she agreed. But she became so frightened to face Amy's father in a trial that she cut her wrists. At that point, we agreed with the doctors that Jannie could not go through with it.

Jannie also asked us not to tell our friends; she needed her privacy. So my husband and I could confide only in our therapists. Once when we saw the abuser on the street, my husband spat at him. We spent many sleepless nights together trying to figure out how to punish this man. For a few years, my husband would go down to the Fulton Fish Market on Sundays and get some dead fish and put them outside the door of his home. He also sent him threatening letters.

I sank deep into a depression and felt I was the worst mother in the world. I felt doubly guilty because we had adopted Jannie. We were so blessed to have her, and then I did not protect her.

A few years after Jannie's breakdown, my husband died—of a second heart attack. He was just fifty-two years old. I believe he simply couldn't live without seeing justice done. I sometimes wish that I could just kill this horrible man myself. I have had thoughts of cutting off his penis and shoving it down his throat. I am still filled with rage and confusion all these years after my daughter was raped.

The good news is that Jannie is a happy person. She is twenty-seven now and working. She has graduated from college, has friends and a social life, and she is not nearly as scarred from this abuse as I am. Thank God.

My Thoughts

Jannie was off at college when Samantha became my client. She has worked very hard in her therapy to try to forgive herself. As she said, her feelings of rage turned inward, into depression, while her husband's turned outward.

Tragically, his rage ended up killing him, or at least hastening his death. He simply could not live with the knowledge that this monster who had brutalized his daughter was free.

Recently, the man and his wife moved away from New York, and the one comfort Samantha has is that neither she nor her daughter will ever have to see him again. This family stood by their daughter, even when it meant not getting the justice they thought she (and they) deserved. Their support was a huge part of what made it possible for Jannie to recover.

Another mother of a fifteen-year-old client and incest survivor had me mesmerized with her extraordinary story. This mother acted like a lioness protecting her young.

For much of Emily's childhood, her parents were both heavy drinkers. Emily had a pretty rough time, but she did feel love from her parents. Her mother entered AA when Emily was ten years old and then divorced her father three years later, when he wouldn't stop drinking. Emily had visits with her father every other weekend. When Emily was fourteen, her parents had a custody hearing because her father wanted more time with his daughter, and Emily told the court officer that on her visits to her father, he had been forcing sex on her. Here is what happened, in her mother's words:

{ *Emily's Mother's Story* }
I'll Kill Him

I was in a drunken fog for many years. Only since I've been sober, for the past four years, have I finally begun to see clearly. I knew my ex-husband was still a drunk, but I never, ever suspected him of molesting our daughter. When Emily told the court officer that she didn't want to visit her father anymore because he was molesting her, you know what I did? I went up to her and slapped her hard across the face. Hmm . . . that was crazy. I was definitely feeling crazy at that moment.

Instead of recoiling or slapping me back, Emily grabbed me and hugged me. She said, "Mom, it's true." Well, I just lost it. I jumped over the courtroom railing and ran to my ex and began to pummel him. The court officers had to pull me off him. Then they wrote up an order of protection for him against me until the sex-abuse allegations were substantiated. As if that weren't outrageous enough, then the court told us that my daughter would have to continue to have visits with her father, but that they would be supervised. I was fit to be tied.

Later that day, my daughter actually went back to school. She was so relieved to have the truth out, she told me she could deal with anything. I went home in a fog. Almost robotically, as if under a hypnotic spell, I went upstairs to my room, took out my (licensed) gun, loaded it (with three bullets, just in case I missed), put on a trench coat, tucked the gun under my coat, and started heading back to my car. I was planning to go to my ex's home and kill him in cold blood. There was no doubt in my mind. He had to die.

Just as I was getting into my car, my sister pulled up in front of my house. Turns out Emily had phoned her, worried about my state. I told my sister that I was on my way to kill my ex because he had molested Emily. Actually I can't really remember exactly what I said. I was blind with rage, but my sister tells me I spoke in a dead monotone. When I told her I was going to kill him, she slapped me, and hard. She explained that I was in shock and needed the slap to snap out of it. We sat down, and she made me give her the gun. Then we both sobbed into each other's arms.

My Thoughts

I treated Emily and her mother for a while. It's been five years since the incident at the court, and Emily's mother never did follow through on her threat. But, as she says, she still lives in a kind of jail—not a typical jail cell, but a jail of guilt for having been so blind. She was an alcoholic and not the mother she should have been. She won't let herself off the hook.

Emily is far better off emotionally than her mother. She is in college and has had therapy. She has close friends and a love for poetry that has helped her to deal with her parents and her upbringing. Emily's father was never put on trial. Emily was just too frightened to go through with it. But they did get her father to sign a legal document stating that he agreed to leave the state, be on probation for the next twelve years, and never contact Emily again.

Through these five years, Emily has not spoken to her father once. She has done a lot of work to heal herself from the abuse, but she says that the most important path to her deep healing was her mother's love and support.

Listen Up, Parents

"When my mother believed me, I knew I would be all right."

—A SIXTEEN-YEAR-OLD SURVIVOR OF MENTOR ABUSE

It is often the case that when sex-abuse survivors see their families begin to deal with feelings of betrayal, their own healing begins. Just the acknowledgment and the support can make a girl begin to feel it's not all her fault. That's why it's so important for parents to show support and to believe in their daughters. But they also have to keep a grip on themselves. Even though they may feel enraged at the violation against their child, even though they may want blood or justice, they have to understand that it was the daughter who was abused, and that her wishes need to be respected. That may mean not talking about the abuse in the extended family. It may mean not going to trial if doing so feels like another violation to a girl.

In the last two stories, one mother went into a serious depression, and the other became homicidal, and one father actually died of a broken heart, but in both stories, the parents understood that their daughters did not feel strong enough to go through the criminal justice system and did not force them to go to trial. That was one of the best ways they could show their support.

In my many years of work, I have witnessed many parents and daughters experience very deep pain. But there are many other ways in which families show support—not just through going to therapy or discussing everything with great emotion. Sometimes a family quietly supports a daughter through its actions. The first action is simply believing their daughter.

Pearl's family was one such family. I met Pearl when she was sixteen years old. She was a new member to our sex-abuse support group and did not speak for the first few weeks. Pearl is a petite Filipino girl from a very strict and religious family. She is quiet and shy and very driven academically. When she finally did share in our group, she said she knew she wanted to protect her sister from their pedophile uncle. Pearl tells a story of a very supportive family who believed her and stood by her, even when it meant defying both their culture—which prizes privacy above all—and their large, extended family.

{ *Pearl's Story* }

Church Songs

I am sixteen years old and Filipino. I was born in the United States, but a lot of my relatives immigrated to the States within the past twenty years. We are a tightly knit family. We celebrate holidays together, we babysit for cousins, we hang out together. I guess you could say our parents depend on each other to keep all our lives running smoothly.

My uncle started molesting me when I was seven years old and continued to do so until I was thirteen. I tried very hard to block out the abuse. I got involved as a peer counselor at school, I was on the honor roll and involved in my church, and I began dating a little. I thought I was fine.

Uncle Jim had always been my favorite uncle, and his daughter, who was five years older than me, had always been like a sister to me. But one day things changed. We were over at his house, and he asked me to come to his room. When I walked in, he was wearing only underpants. That was already weird for me, considering my parents' modesty, and I was pretty scared. Then he asked me to come closer to him. Reluctantly, I approached him. He took out his penis and put it in my hand. It felt disgusting. I wanted to die. But I stood there paralyzed. Then he put it in my mouth. He said it wasn't going to hurt. He told me not to be afraid and said that he loved me. Then he said, "This is our little secret."

After that I tried to avoid him, but several times he came to my school to pick me up, telling my teacher that my parents had sent him. I didn't want to make a scene, so I just got in the back seat of his car. But then he'd take out his penis and begin masturbating. He'd keep telling me how special I was, and that he loved me, and that I should touch him. I'd just sit there, frozen, looking out the window and trying to blank out until he dropped me off at home.

He used to bring me gifts and money in front of my parents, and of course I accepted them. I wish I had never accepted anything from him. This is one reason I feel so guilty. To this day, it really bothers me that I accepted his gifts. He never threatened my life, but I was afraid of him. His words were very powerful. I knew that what was going on was extremely wrong, but I wasn't sure how to stop it. Mostly I wanted to get away from him, but the little part of me that felt special wanted to stay, and I kept thinking maybe he would stop. I guess that is why I felt so responsible for and guilty about what happened.

By the time I turned thirteen, I could no longer be in a room with him without feeling sick. My body had started to develop, and I'd started getting my period. Maybe unconsciously I felt the beginnings of womanhood. Whatever it was, I started taking action. I told Uncle Jim he could not be alone with me. He became really nasty and threatened to "get me" when I wasn't looking. But I stayed away from him. I hated and feared him.

I began to have dreams about my uncle. I would wake up in a cold sweat of fear. Then the smell of cigarettes started triggering all these awful feelings and memories. I remembered how it used to feel when he'd touch me or whisper in my ear. I'd think about how he used to make these disgusting gestures. And it all came back to me. A week after hearing Patti speak at my school about sexual abuse, we had a family celebration. As always, my uncle tried to hug me too tightly, and after I wrenched out of his embrace, I saw him hugging my twelve-year-old sister the same way. Then, right before my eyes, I saw him touch her breast. I knew then and there that I had to stop him. When my uncle started molesting my little sister, I had a choice: to save her or keep my extended family together. I chose to save my sister.

I tried to think of ways to stop him from getting to my sister. I wanted to tell my parents but I didn't know how. My parents and I were always pretty close. My parents are traditional in lots of ways and very conservative about sexuality. As much as I love them, I am very aware of pleasing them and being a "good girl." So there are lots of things I don't tell my mom, and the sexual abuse was one of them. But it always felt like this huge, ugly secret.

When Dr. Patti came to my school and started talking about sexual abuse, she explained that it is never the child's fault. For the first time, I began to realize that maybe my uncle had been manipulating me all that time, and that he was entirely to blame. I was ready to tell my secret. It was hard for me to talk in the sexual-abuse support groups, but after hearing all these horrible stories from these other girls, too, I felt I could share my experience. Hearing so many other girls who I never would have dreamed were abused made me feel less alone. You could just tell from their stories that their abuse wasn't their fault. Maybe mine wasn't my fault, either.

On my sixteenth birthday, I went to see the counselor at my school, with the support of Patti and the other girls behind me. I knew I could do it. I knew from Patti that when I told my counselor he would call the police—because the abuse happened less than six years ago and involved two minors, the school had to report it—but I knew I had to do something. When I told him, of course, he said he'd have to get the principal. I was so scared and upset. I didn't know what was going to happen. I asked my friends to stay with me.

The next thing I knew, the police showed up at my school. They talked with me and asked me lots of questions, and then they called my parents. My father came to the school. His just being there, so awkward, so out of his element, was startling enough for me. But then, with the help of my counselor and principal, I told my father about my uncle, and my father began to cry. I had never seen him cry before. He asked me why I hadn't told them. I told him I was scared, and by then I was sobbing, too. I felt so ashamed that I couldn't look at him. I was sure he thought of me as less of a person.

At home, my mother made me feel much worse. She didn't say anything; she just looked at me in horror, and then she slapped my face. Thankfully, she called a close family friend for support, and when her friend came over, she told my mother that she had been sexually abused by her brother-in-law when she was a teenager and had attempted suicide. Then my mother looked me in the eye with a new understanding, and I knew that she believed me. At that moment, I felt my mother's love. But I also knew that she could not deal with what was happening.

The next few hours were very intense. My mother called Uncle Jim's wife, her sister, and told her what had happened. My aunt said she did not believe me. While they were on the phone, the police arrived at my uncle's place of work, and he was taken to the police station for questioning. While all this was going on, I could hardly look at my parents. My father was crying, and my mother was shaking all over. My poor little sister came home to all this pandemonium. When she found out what was going on, she said that Uncle Jim had given her the creeps for a long time.

Needless to say, family relations were severely strained. My aunt and cousin sided with my uncle. My mother stopped calling her sister, and my cousin wouldn't speak to me. I felt like I had lost my older sister. My dad seemed really embarrassed around me, and my mother tried very hard not to hold anything against me, but there were times when she would just look at me and shake her head and say, "How did this happen? How did you not tell me?"

My sister came to me and said, "Thank you, Pearl. You know, I've always been kind of disgusted by Uncle Jim, but I thought it was my imagination that he was touching my breast when he hugged me. I didn't know he had touched you, but I was really scared." Hearing my sister's words made it all worth it to me. I could give up my relationship with my cousin. I could even live with my mother's ambivalence if I managed to save my sister from Uncle Jim's abuse.

It's been a year since I disclosed the abuse to my family. I am seventeen now, and a lot has changed for me. I don't think about my uncle as much, and when I do, I know how to deal with the feelings that come up through journal-writing, going to group, and doing these relaxation exercises Patti taught me. I still have a lot of feelings about what happened with my uncle, but the strongest emotion is not fear. I still don't speak to my cousin, but I am not as sad about it as I was a year ago. I sleep better. I feel happier. I feel so relieved that I don't have to worry anymore about anyone finding out. All the important people in my life know. I am not hiding anything anymore. It really feels like a weight I have been carrying around is off my shoulders.

My dad never talks about the abuse. My mom sometimes mumbles that she wishes she could see her sister, and sometimes she even slips and blames me for letting things with my uncle go on for so long. But last week in church I felt my mother reach for my hand while singing her favorite hymn, and it felt so real to me. We don't have this huge secret between us anymore.

My Thoughts

Pearl's is a success story in many ways, but her family's support was certainly key to her healing. Although they had to go through some difficult feelings to get there, they stood by Pearl, even when it meant losing connections with important family members. Although Pearl had haunting memories of her abuse, those memories led her to get help. It's even somewhat surprising that her mother and father were so fully supportive and willing to confront the uncle. Most Asian cultures strenuously protect the family image and guard family secrets. Also, in the cultural hierarchy, boys are more respected than girls, and we might have expected her parents to try to hide Pearl's abuse to protect the honor of her respected uncle. He was one of the first family members to immigrate to the United States and was held in very high esteem. That's why it's all the more remarkable that Pearl's parents were willing to become estranged from him and the extended family. Filipino women tend to go to great pains to make sure that the men "look good" to the world and in the community, and Filipino, as well as many Spanish, families will go to great lengths to avoid *chismosa*, or gossip, about the family.

Of course, Pearl will never forget her mother's slap, but it seems that in that act, her mother released her anger and shock and then was able to face Pearl. Her father simply never discusses the abuse. Although the Filipino culture is considered a matriarchy, girls and women are taught to defer to boys and men, especially in the family. Parents of many cultural persuasions are often eager to deny that their child has been abused, especially by a relative. It just brings up too many tricky emotions.

One of the things many girls have told me is that it often isn't until their parents can look them in the eye again that they feel they can look in the mirror. Girls can stay stuck in their shame when their parents are stuck in their own grief, shock, despair, and pity. Daughters need to know that they are not the three Ds: dirty, damaged, defective. They need their parents to be able to look them in the eye—and work out their discomfort away from their daughters—so that they can help their daughters feel all right in their own skins again.

In her book *Lucky*, Alice Sebold talks about her first encounter with her mother after she had to phone her and tell her she had been brutally raped by a stranger in the park the night before. She said that when she saw her mother, with all her fresh energy, she knew she could handle things and get through the rest of the day.

Ironically, young women can rebound from trauma more quickly than their loving parents do. But it is the loving parents who speed up the healing, just through their love.

Chapter 13

Finding Your Support Posse

When you are a survivor of sexual abuse, and especially of incest, trust is hard to come by. You can start to believe that no one in the world will help you. Your abuser has blamed you or convinced you that what he is doing is right. Just as Coral's father told her, men tell girls that sex is a rite of passage, "like a Bat Mitzvah." You may feel too isolated to know that there really is help and support out there.

As strange as it may seem to you, most families would be completely devastated if their daughters were abused, and, frankly, so would most people. For all the crass commercials and obscene music videos out there, there's also a tremendous movement against the tide of abuse, and it's beginning to work. By telling your truth, you are adding force to that movement. There are more women judges, more women lawyers, more feminists, both male and female, in the criminal justice system, and more advocates for children. And more people than ever are willing to speak out loud and in public about sexual abuse.

We are also seeing more and more grassroots efforts at change—from individuals to organizations, schools, hospitals, crisis centers, and websites. As I see it, each of these represents a piece of that mosaic we spoke about earlier—the incredible mosaic of our movement to combat sexual abuse.

There are women and men, mothers and fathers, teachers and counselors, nurses, doctors, and lawyers across the country reaching out to young people, trying to make a difference. There are rape crisis centers at most colleges and universities. There are groups for survivors, as well as individual counseling. And as sexist as much of the music culture is, some feminist musicians have come out with songs about their abuse, including Tori Amos, who started the Rape, Abuse, and Incest National Network (RAINN), and Ani DiFranco, who sings about women's empowerment and started her own record label, Righteous Babe Records, because she would not be packaged by the corporate music industry.

Boys Will Be Boys . . . Not Always

Even some men from major rock bands have come forward to take a very vocal stand against rape. At the 1999 MTV Music Awards, the Beastie Boys condemned Limp Bizkit for the several rapes that happened at Woodstock 1999. They attributed the rapes to the lyrics of a Limp Bizkit song played at the festival that actually encouraged men to rape women. The Red Hot Chili Peppers have taken a stand, too, through their support of RAINN, which, by the way, has a man for president! Film director Tim Roth has also championed the issue of sexual abuse of girls. His movie *The War Zone* was about a boy who wanted to kill his father for molesting his sister.

Boys and young men are under tremendous pressure to adopt the role of the "mack daddy." Those boys who want sincere friendships with girls—who, like most girls, just want to take things slow and have the time and space to explore their sexuality, and who don't just want to "fuck"—are put down as wimps.

There are young men volunteering at rape crisis hotlines and escorting girls on campuses when there are rape scares. And more and more fathers are respecting their wives and daughters as equals and taking pride in their daughters' physical strength and accomplishments.

Yes, we have a long way to go in changing our sexist culture, but many people out there are helping us move to a better place. They are doing so in response to the outrageous truths that girls and women have been willing to share. Every time a survivor breaks open the taboo of sexual abuse and speaks out, she helps the culture of boys and men by teaching everyone what sexual abuse does to a person, the pain that's involved. This is a bottom-up movement all the way.

☼   ☼   ☼

Life Goes On

You may never be able to heal the damage done in your family. You may hate your abuser forever; you may struggle with forgiving your mother for letting the incest happen. You may even need to separate from your family and create a new one. Girls often have to create new families and new support systems that they can count on as they move forward in their lives.

But please know that help is out there. You'll be surprised by how many people will join you in your anger at your abuser, join you in your healing process. Yes, getting your posse together can take time. You sometimes need great patience. But don't give up. If at first you don't get the response you are looking for from the people you tell, find others. Join a survivors' group. Talk to an aunt or a cousin or someone you know you can really trust. Call a hotline. You will find your support system.

All sexual-abuse survivors are righteous and strong. You are beautiful. Your abuse is just a part of you, a part of your past. It does not define you. It is something that was done to you. You cannot undo it, but you can heal from it and lead a wonderful, blessed life filled with success, love, fulfillment, power, creativity, and healing. There are people out there who will help you—good people who will love you and whom you will love. Together, you will move out of the darkness of abuse into the light of life.

Epilogue

Invisible No More

This book was ten years in the making. Over the course of these years, many of the girls whose stories were shared in the book have come back to see me. Even though many have moved to different states, and some even to different countries, we've stayed in touch. They have grown, changed, and gotten beyond their abuse. I was the first person many of these beautiful girls shared their experiences with. It's a strong link that connects us, even if we are out of touch.

I thought I'd update you on a few of the girls. There is life after sexual abuse. I see it every day. And here's your chance to see it with me:

Sage, the topless dancer, came to see me five years after our therapy ended. She'd moved to another state, gotten married, and had a baby. At the time of her visit, she was twenty-nine and working part-time teaching art to children. Seeing her doing so well, I was overwhelmed with joy that generations of abuse in Sage's family had stopped, and I was so moved when Sage let me hold her daughter. She said, "Patti, I can't tell you how much joy I get from my daughter and the knowledge that she'll never be abused like I was."

Lily, the girl who survived abuse by imagining herself to be a superhero, called me a few years ago about her first social work case. She had successfully fought to have an abused victim removed from her abuser-father's home and was feeling really good about her work.

Coral, whose father raped her for so many years in Holland, is happily married with twin daughters and three cats. She and her husband are restoring their historical home in Vermont.

Iris, who was date-raped by the college boy she thought was so cute, published her first collection of poetry, and one poem talked about her rape and the long journey to love that followed.

Garnet, the girl whose father raped both her and her sister, came back a couple of years after she wrote her story. Her sister, who, you'll recall, had been living on the streets as a prostitute, is now living with Garnet and her husband and has decided to join Garnet in pursuing charges against their father.

Dahlia, who was gang-raped and spent years battling anorexia, has started volunteering at a rape hotline while she is in graduate school pursuing a career in journalism.

Zinnia, who escaped her torture by cataloguing flowers and building beautiful homes in the woods, is happily coupled with another woman, and they live and work together with their three cats and two dogs in a farmhouse in Montana.

Amber, who suffered from acquaintance abuse at her camp when she was twelve, just gave birth to a healthy baby boy and lives and works in Paris with her husband.

All these girls have found strength in becoming visible. They have told their truths. Every time a girl comes forward with her truth, opening Pandora's box with her story of sexual abuse, she too becomes visible. By telling your story, you not only ensure your own healing but also help other girls to come forward. Together, we are inching our way toward a future when men can no longer get away with sexually abusing girls and women.

It's possible. I just know it is. As that wise eighteen-year-old said earlier, you can transform that pile of shit into a patch of daisies.

Endnotes

Chapter 6
The Deepest Wound: *Father-Daughter Incest*

[1] From a January 2000 interview with Kay Jackson, a psychologist who specializes in treating pedophiles.

Chapter 8
Trusting the Wrong Men:
Abuse by Teachers, Coaches, Clergy

[1] See writ.news.findlaw.com/hamilton/20041230.html for a review of the legal landscape regarding clegy abuse.

Chapter 10
Rape Always Hurts: *Stranger Rape, Date Rape, Gang Rape*

[1] According to the Bureau of Justice Statistics Criminal Victimization Survey, 2002

[2] *Sexual Violence on Campus Policies, Programs, and Perspectives* Allen J. Ottens-Kathy Hotelling Springer Series on Family Violence 2001.

[3] Humphrey, S., and A. Kahn (2000). "Fraternities, Athletic Teams and Rape: Importance of Identification with a Risky Group." *Journal of Interpersonal Violence*, as cited in U.S. Dept. of Justice Office of Community-Oriented Policing Services Acquaintance Rape of College Students by Rana Simpson, no. 17.

[4] Three percent as cited in the Report on the Sexual Victimization of College Women (2001) by the Justice Department's National Institute of Justice and Bureau of Justice Statistics; 25 percent as reported by B. Fisher and J. Sloan III (1995). *Campus Crime: Legal, Social and Policy Perspectives.* Springfield, IL: Charles C. Thomas.

[5] According to *Ms.* magazine online, summer 2004 edition: "India, Malaysia, Tonga, Ethiopia, Lebanon, Guatemala, and Uruguay exempt men from penalty for rape—if they subsequently marry their victims." Once they are married, there is, from a legal standpoint, no such thing as rape.

[6] According to Robin Warshaw, *I Never Called It Rape* (NY: Harper Perennial, 1994). 75 percent of the men and 55 percent of the women involved in date rape had been drinking or taking drugs before the attack occurred.

[7] According to B. Fisher and J. Sloan III (1995) *Campus Crime: Legal, Social and Policy Perspectives* (Springfield, IL: Charles C. Thomas), fewer than 5 percent of college women who are victims of rape or attempted rape report it to police. According to the Bureau of Justice Statistics National Crime Victimization Survey, only 39 percent of rapes and sexual assaults are reported to law-enforcement officials—about one in every three. This strikes me as a very high estimate.

[8] According to the National Center for Policy Analysis, probability statistics compiled from U.S. Dept. of Justice statistics suggest that only one out of sixteen rapists will ever spend a day in jail.

[9] From www.nd.edu/~ucc/ucc_sexualvictimhospital.html

There's Help Out There

The Resource Center

This resource section is here to educate, enlighten, and resonate. I want girls—and all those in contact with girls—to get help and become smarter about sexual abuse, so I have included educators and parents in this audience. I have read most of the books out there on this subject, and in this resource section, I give you the best of the best, including both classics and cutting-edge books and a mix of books, websites, and hotlines for you to explore. There is a world out there for girls to tap into, and with each exploration comes visibility.

Teen Counseling Books for Parents and Adolescent Girls

Dating Violence: Young Women in Danger
by Barrie Levy. Seattle, WA: Seal Press, 1991.

Features twenty brief but powerful first-person accounts from abused teens or their mothers.

How Long Does it Hurt?: A Guidebook to Recovering from Incest and Sexual Abuse for Teenagers, Their Friends, and Their Families
by Cynthia Mather and Kristina Debye. San Francisco, CA: Jossey-Bass, 2004.

This is a step-by-step recovery guide for teenagers who are faced with sexual abuse. Lots of practical advice on knowing who to tell, getting safe, feeling comfortable with your sexuality, going to court, and interacting with your family and friends as you recover.

In Love & in Danger: A Teen's Guide to Breaking Free of Abusive Relationships
by Barrie Levy. Seattle, WA: Seal Press, 1997.

This book, directed at teenagers, includes teens' stories and advice from Levy. Helpful topics include sex-abuse and relationship abuse.

Kids Helping Kids Break the Silence of Sexual Abuse
by Linda Lee Foltz. Pittsburgh, PA: Lighthouse Point Press, 2003.

Each chapter of this book shares the true story of a child victim of sexual abuse. These stories are about breaking the bonds of silence and getting help and will be of interest to survivors, parents, and counselors.

The Me Nobody Knows: A Guide for Teen Survivors
by Barbara Bean and Shari Bennett. New York, NY: Lexington Books, 1993.

This book is geared toward recovering teens and talks about the conflicting emotions that often result from an experience with sexual abuse.

Saving Beauty from the Beast: How to Protect Your Daughter from an Unhealthy Relationship
by Vicki Crompton and Ellen Zelda Kessner.
Boston, MA: Little, Brown & Co., 2003.

This is aimed at parents of teenage daughters.

Who to Turn To: Helping Resources and Organizations, Hotlines, and Websites

These organizations can give you guidance and advice, direct you to counseling and resources in your area, and, in many cases, provide you with concrete services.

❊   ❊   ❊

Childhelp USA
(800) 4-A-CHILD (1-800-422-4453)
National Child Abuse Hotline
www.childhelpusa.org

National Domestic Violence Hotline
(800) 799-SAFE (799-7233)
www.ndvh.org

National Hopeline Network
(800) SUICIDE (784-2433)
www.hopeline.com

National Office of Victim Assistance
(800) TRY-NOVA

National Runaway Switchboard
(800) 621-4000

National STD/HIV Hotline
(800) 227-8922

The National Women's Health Information Center
www.4woman.gov/faq/sexualassault.htm

National Youth Crisis Hotline
National Youth Development
(800) HIT-HOME (448-4663)
Referral hotline for youths 17 and under

Rape, Abuse, and Incest National Network (RAINN)
National Sexual Assault Hotline
(800) 656-4673
www.rainn.org

Professional Advocacy Organizations

American Professional Society on the Abuse of Children (APSAC)
www.apsac.org

An interdisciplinary society for professionals working in the field of child abuse and neglect.

Child Abuse Prevention Network
www.childabuse.com

The Internet nerve center for professionals in the field of child abuse and neglect.

Children's Bureau Express
http://cbexpress.acf.hhs.gov

Designed for professionals concerned with child abuse and neglect, child welfare, and adoption. It is rich with publications, abstracts, primary research, news, and more.

Generation Five
www.generationfive.org

Generation Five is a nonprofit organization that brings together diverse community leaders working to end child sexual abuse within five generations.

International Society for Prevention of Child Abuse and Neglect
www.ispcan.org

ISPCAN's mission is to prevent cruelty to children in every nation, in every form: physical abuse, sexual abuse, neglect, street children, child fatalities, child prostitution, children of war, emotional abuse, and child labor.

NYC Alliance Against Sexual Assault
www.nycagainstrape.org

The mission of the New York City Alliance Against Sexual Assault is to advocate that survivors receive appropriate support and intervention by uniting organizations, influencing policy, and promoting advocacy, education, and research.

Pennsylvania Coalition Against Rape

www.teenpcar.com

A great source for teens. On the website, you'll find tips for boys and girls, plus references for getting help and getting involved in the fight against sexual violence.

Prevent Child Abuse New York

www.preventchildabuseny.org

PCANY helps families, professionals, and community members to improve parenting practices and to prevent and intervene in child abuse and neglect. The first line of defense against child abuse is good parenting, so PCANY focuses heavily on serving parents, as well as professionals who work with parents and children. The website has useful resources for kids, parents, professionals, and advocates. New Yorkers can call the parent hotline at (800) 342-7472.

Promote Truth

www.promotetruth.org

The mission of Promote Truth is to provide support and information about sexual violence issues for teens and their communities. Promote Truth was created by the Rape Recovery Team at the Women's Center of Jacksonville in Florida.

SIECUS

www.siecus.org

SIECUS (Sexuality Information and Education Council of the United States) is a clearinghouse of sexuality information, giving girls access to medically accurate, comprehensive information about sexuality and reproductive health issues.

STAAR

http://dolphin.upenn.edu/~staar/

STAAR (Students Together Against Acquaintance Rape) is a university site set up by students and a peer-health education program dedicated to educating the Penn campus about the problem of acquaintance rape and sexual violence in general.

Therapistfinder Child Abuse Information

www.therapistfinder.net/Child-Abuse

These pages provide thorough and helpful information on child abuse, including federal definitions of child abuse, signs of child abuse, statistics, effects, treatments, and resources.

Legal Resources

To Report Suspected Child Abuse

Each state designates specific agencies to receive and investigate reports of suspected child abuse and neglect. Typically, this responsibility is carried out by child protective services (CPS) within a Department of Social Services, Department of Human Resources, or Division of Family and Children Services. In some states, police departments may also receive reports of child abuse or neglect. For more information or assistance with reporting, please call Childhelp USA, (800) 4-A-CHILD (422-4453), or your local CPS agency. The National Clearinghouse on Child Abuse and Neglect Information has compiled a state-by-state list of child-abuse reporting contact information (see listing below).

Association of Child Abuse Lawyers (ACAL)

www.childabuselawyers.com

Practical support for survivors and professionals working in the field of abuse.

Child Abuse Legislation Study Project

www.childabuselegislation.org

Information about state legislation and enforcement of sexual-abuse laws.

National Center for Prosecution of Child Abuse

www.ndaa-apri.org/apri/programs/ncpca/ncpca_home.html

Aimed at responding to an increase in reported child abuse, the National Center serves as a central resource for training, expert legal assistance, court reform, and state-of-the-art information on criminal child abuse investigations and prosecutions. They provide training and technical assistance, a clearinghouse on child abuse case law, statutory initiatives, court reforms and trial strategies, authoritative publications, and primary research on state and federal developments, best practices, and prosecutorial innovations.

National Center for Victims of Crime

www.ncvc.org/ncvc/

The National Center for Victims of Crime is dedicated to forging a national commitment to help victims of crime rebuild their lives. The National Center's toll-free helpline, (800) FYI-CALL (394-2255), offers supportive counseling, practical information about crime and victimization, referrals to local community resources, and skilled advocacy in the criminal justice and social service systems.

National Clearinghouse on Child Abuse and Neglect Information (NCCAN)

http://nccanch.acf.hhs.gov/

NCCAN provides access to the most extensive, up-to-date collection of information on child abuse and neglect in the world. An extraordinarily thorough resource.

Empowerment: Surviving and Thriving
Reclaiming Our Sexuality

Advocates for Youth

www.advocatesforyouth.org

Online resources for teens, parents, and professionals on adolescent sexual and reproductive health.

The Body

www.thebody.com/safesex/safer.html

Comprehensive website on safe sex—lots of great information.

Scarleteen

www.scarleteen.com/

A comprehensive sex education site for teens, covering everything from STDs to sexual abuse. Scarleteen is owned by Scarlet Letters, an adult women's sexuality journal.

Sex, Etc.

www.sexetc.org

Launched in 1994 with the help of two health educators and a professional journalist, Sex, Etc. is a sexuality and health newsletter written by teens for teens, covering issues from dating, to STDs.

Our Bodies, Ourselves for the New Century
by the Boston Women's Health Book Collective.
New York, NY: Simon & Schuster, 1998.

Probably the most complete book on teen sexuality. This is the teen version of the revolutionary feminist classic *Our Bodies, Ourselves*, and includes invaluable information on bodies and sexuality, with plenty of diagrams.

Body Outlaws: Rewriting the Rules of Beauty and Body Image
edited by Ophira Edut. Emeryville, CA: Seal Press, 2003.

This book offers many vignettes from young women who write about their body image, some from a feminist perspective. This book offers girls an alternative to the standard measurements of beauty.

A Girl's Guide to Taking Over the World:
Writings from the Girl Zine Revolution
edited by Karen Green and Tristan Taormino.
New York, NY: St. Martin's Griffin, 1997.

This collection, like the zines themselves, gives voice to real opinions that young women's magazines like *YM*, *Seventeen*, and *Jane* only hope to emulate.

Ophelia Speaks: Adolescent Girls Write About Their Search for Self
by Sara Shandler. New York, NY: HarperPerennial, 1999.

Sara Shandler edited this when she was eighteen years old. It includes short vignettes written by teen girls on topics like sexuality, eating disorders, depression, and sexual abuse.

Websites and Magazines

Bitch: Feminist Response to Pop Culture

www.bitchmagazine.com

Bitch is a print magazine that critiques TV, movies, magazines, and ads from a feminist perspective.

Bust

www.bust.com

Bust is a print magazine that offers an "uncensored view on the female experience." Visit the site for articles, links to the girl wide web, shopping, discussions, chats, and more.

By Girls for Girls

www.bygirlsforgirls.org

By Girls for Girls is a lovely site set up for girls written by the teens themselves. This site talks about teen dating violence and provides advice and resources.

Communities Against Rape and Abuse

www.cara-seattle.org/youth.html

CARA is a resource for young people who want to create support for young survivors of rape and abuse, as well as young people who want to work to end all forms of violence and oppression through activism and community organizing.

Feminist.com

www.feminist.com

Loads of resources for girls, including sections on activism and anti-violence resources.

Feminist Majority

www.feminist.org

This website for the Feminist Majority Foundation gives information on feminist news and events, opportunities for activism, a feminist career center, and great links and products.

Girlthrive

www.girlthrive.com

This website is designed for teen girls and young women who have survived sexual abuse, with information, stories, and expert interviews.

Hardy Girls Healthy Women

www.hardygirlshealthywomen.org

Hardy Girls Healthy Women is a site started by Lyn Mikel Brown and her partners to help young girls begin to find positive ways to grow and learn in "hardiness zones," located in Maine.

Ms.

www.msmagazine.com

Ms. magazine was "the first national magazine to make feminist voices audible, feminist journalism tenable, and a feminist worldview available to the public." Visit the website for a wealth of resources, stories, and links.

National Organization for Women (NOW)

www.now.org

The National Organization for Women (NOW) is the largest organization of feminist activists in the United States.

TeenWire

www.teenwire.com/index.asp

A website for teens needing information about sexual health. Information on sexual health, self-esteem, body image, drugs and alcohol, communication, and relationship advice, sponsored by Planned Parenthood. Also available in Spanish through the *en español* section of the site.

Teen Voices

http://teenvoices.com

A magazine for, by, and about teenage and young adult women. Includes features on arts, the media, politics, and teen issues, plus an advice column, personal essays, poetry, and fiction.

Youth Connections

www.youthcomm.org

New Youth Connections (or NYC) is a general-interest teen magazine written by and for New York City youth, covering topics from sex abuse and rape to adoption and family issues.

Novels/Memoirs of Survivors

Many novels and autobiographical memoirs about survivors are available. Many of them are about severe and brutal abuse. The books I have listed are more about the aftereffects and inner experience of the survivors, rather than the brutal abuse. These books are powerful for young women. Many of them are written in the voice of an adolescent or young woman.

After Silence: Rape and My Journey Back
by Nancy Venable Raine. New York, NY: Crown, 1998.

This is a book about stranger rape and the author's account of her rape ten years later. It is written almost as a journal and explores the aftereffects of this rape.

Bastard out of Carolina
by Dorothy Allison. New York, NY: Plume, 1993.

Beautifully told story of Bone, a young girl growing up in the rural South amidst violence and sexual abuse, with a heartbreaking mother/daughter relationship. Made into a 1996 movie, directed by Anjelica Huston and starring Jennifer Jason Leigh and Jena Malone.

Childhood's Thief: One Woman's Journey of Healing from Sexual Abuse
by Rose Mary Evans. New York, NY: Bantam Books, 1995.

A wonderful book about severe childhood sexual, verbal, physical, emotional abuse in the 1940s, told years later in the voice of the heroine's therapist. A wonderful, uplifting love takes place in this book.

Fifth Born
by Zelda Lockhart. New York, NY: Atria Books, 2003.

Novel about a young African American girl dealing with family violence and abuse in 1970s Missouri and Mississippi.

I Know Why the Caged Bird Sings
by Maya Angelou. New York, NY: Random House, 2002.

This is a beautiful novel about growing up, and part of its focus (not all) is on incest with the heroine's uncle.

Katie.com: My Story
by Katherine Tarbox. New York, NY: Plume, 2001.

True story of a girl assaulted by a man she met in an Internet chat room.

The Lovely Bones
by Alice Sebold. Boston, MA: Little, Brown & Co., 2002.

The story of Susie Salmon at age fourteen after her death. Susie tells her story from heaven and watches her family deal with her death. There is some recounting of brutal sex abuse and murder. Haunting yet hopeful.

Lucky
by Alice Sebold. New York, NY: Little, Brown & Co., 2002.

Gritty and gripping story of the author's rape during her freshman year of college and the process of bringing her rapist to justice.

My Father's House: A Memoir of Incest and Healing
by Sylvia Fraser. New York, NY: Perennial Library, 1989.

A powerful, harrowing memoir of an incestuous relationship between a father and a daughter, beginning in the mid-1930s. The writing is very graphic and extremely disturbing, but the book is written in a way that engages and ends with healing.

Spread Your Wings and Fly: A Teenager's Journey of Suspense, Romance and Terror (in Overcoming Sexual Abuse)
by Rebecca Engle Smith. Salt Lake City, UT: Agreka Books, 2000.

Fact-based fictional account of a teenage girl dealing with sexual abuse and the ups and downs of adolescence.

Stella Landry
by Robin McCorquodale. New York, NY: Morrow, 1992.

A beautiful fiction book about a young mid-century Texas woman who endured abuse and came out on the other side.

Where I Stopped: Remembering an Adolescent Rape
by Martha Ramsey. San Diego, CA: Harcourt Brace, 1997.

An autobiographical novel that tells the story of a thirteen-year-old girl and her stranger-rape experience. The book documents the aftermath and recovery and is very readable.

Films

Bastard out of Carolina (1996)
directed by Anjelica Huston.

Based on the autobiographical novel written by Dorothy Allison, this is a heartwrenching film in which a mother rejects her daughter for her abusive husband.

Lipstick (1976)
directed by Lamont Johnson.

A movie about teacher abuse and sisterly loyalties and protectiveness.

Loyalties (1999)
directed by Lesley Ann Patten.

A Canadian film made by a woman filmmaker. Very supportive to women, with extraordinary scenes of a mother and her fifteen-year-old daughter.

Monsoon Wedding (2001)
directed by Mira Nair.

An all-around beautiful film that includes one of the most wonderful examples of family support surrounding incest. Also directed by a woman.

Nuts (1987)
directed by Martin Ritt.

Barbara Streisand stars in this amazing film about incest. One of the most realistic caricatures of the incest mother.

Clinical and Educational Books on Rape, Incest, and Sexual Abuse

Against Our Will: Men, Women, and Rape
by Susan Brownmiller. New York, NY: Fawcett Columbine, 1993.

This is one of the most important books around on rape and injustice to women.

Allies in Healing: When the Person
You Love Was Sexually Abused as a Child
by Laura Davis. New York, NY: HarperPerennial, 1991.

This is a classic, filled with information, support, and guidance for partners of survivors.

Breaking Down the Wall of Silence:
The Liberating Experience of Facing Painful Truth
by Alice Miller. New York, NY: Meridian, 1997.

Alice Miller, a German psychoanalyst and child advocate, tries to reveal truths about abuse and injustice to all children.

The Courage to Heal: A Guide for Women
Survivors of Child Sexual Abuse
by Ellen Bass and Laura Davis. New York, NY: HarperPerennial, 1994.

This seminal book breaks open the taboo of sex abuse for women.

※   ※   ※

Father-Daughter Incest
by Judith Lewis Herman. Cambridge, MA: Harvard University Press, 2000.

This is an important and groundbreaking book on father-daughter incest from a feminist perspective.

**I Will Survive: The African American Guide
to Healing from Sexual Assault and Abuse**
by Lori Robinson. New York, NY: Seal Press, 2002.

This resource for survivors and their supporters discusses various levels of healing, with particular attention to the recovery process of African American women.

Secret Survivors: Uncovering Incest and Its Aftereffects in Women
by E. Sue Blume. New York, NY: Wiley, 1990.

This book provides an aftereffects checklist and covers the many emotions that can occur post-incest.

The Secret Trauma: Incest in the Lives of Girls and Women
by Diana E.H. Russell. New York, NY: Basic Books, 1986.

This is an excellent book, with some of the first statistics on incest. Filled with history and useful information.

**Trauma and Recovery: The Aftermath of Violence—
from Domestic Abuse to Political Terror**
by Judith Lewis Herman. New York, NY: Basic Books, 1997.

A psychology classic about how violence in all forms affects its survivors. Herman compares the effects of trauma on war prisoners to sex-abuse survivors, again from a feminist perspective.

Patti Feuereisen

Patti Feuereisen, PhD, a psychologist in private practice in Brooklyn Heights and Manhattan, is a pioneer in the treatment of sexual abuse for adolescent girls and young women. She also speaks widely on this topic at high schools and colleges, and for professional associations. Her website, www.girlthrive.com, has become an important international resource for sexual-abuse survivors. Patti Feuereisen holds a doctorate in psychology. She lives in Brooklyn, New York, with her husband, their daughter, and dog Chancey.

Caroline Pincus

Caroline Pincus has been developing and collaborating on nonfiction books for more than twenty years. A longtime acquisitions editor at Harper-Collins in San Francisco, Caroline is passionately committed to books that empower women and girls. She lives in San Francisco, California, with her daughter and wife.

A portion of the proceeds from the sale of this book will benefit Girlthrive, an educational resource for sexual-abuse survivors and college scholarship fund for incest survivors, established by Dr. Patti in 2003 and fiscally supported by RAINN. You can write to Dr. Patti directly through her website, www.girlthrive.com. You'll also find chat rooms, links, interviews with people active in the movement to stop sexual abuse, and lots of other resources on abuse and survival.

Selected Titles from Seal Press

For more than twenty-five years, Seal Press has published groundbreaking books. By women. For women. Visit our website at www.sealpress.com.

Real Girl Real World: A Guide to Finding Your True Self
by Heather M. Gray and Samantha Phillips. $15.95, 1-58005-133-2.

In this fun and essential guide, real girls and teens share their experiences while the authorss discuss beauty and the media; body image and self-esteem; eating disorders and good nutrition; and sex and ways to stay safe and healthy.

**I Will Survive: The African-American Guide
to Healing from Sexual Assault and Abuse**
by Lori S. Robinson. $15.95, 1-58005-080-8.

This valuable resource for survivors—and their families, friends, and communities—walks readers through the processes of emotional, physical, sexual, and spiritual healing and the particular difficulties African Americans face on their journey to recovery.

**In Love & in Danger: A Teen's Guide
to Breaking Free of Abusive Relationships**
by Barrie Levy. $10.95, 1-58005-002-6.

This clear and compassionate guide speaks directly to teens about what constitutes abusive relationships—emotional, physical, and sexual—and how to break free of them.

Listen Up: Voices from the Next Feminist Generation
edited by Barbara Findlen. $16.95, 1-58005-054-9.

A revised and expanded edition of the Seal Press classic, this anthology features the voices of a new generation of women, expressing the vibrancy and vitality of today's feminist movement.

You Can Be Free: An Easy-to-Read Handbook for Abused Women
by Ginny NiCarthy, M.S.W. and Sue Davidson. $10.95, 1-878067-06-0.

A simplified version of *Getting Free, You Can Be Free* is written in an accessible style for the woman in crisis. It covers a range of topics designed to help women leave abusive relationships.

Body Outlaws: Rewriting the Rules of Beauty and Body Image
edited by Ophira Edut, foreword by Rebecca Walker. $15.95, 1-58005-108-1

'⁌d with honesty and humor, this groundbreaking anthology offers stories by
⁀vho have chosen to ignore, subvert, or redefine the dominant beauty stan-
⁀ to feel at home in their bodies.